EFFECTIVE
LEADERSHIP
for NONPROFIT
ORGANIZATIONS

EFFECTIVE LEADERSHIP
for NONPROFIT
ORGANIZATIONS

HOW EXECUTIVE DIRECTORS
AND BOARDS WORK TOGETHER

THOMAS WOLF

Allworth Press • New York

Allworth Press books may be purchased in bulk at special discounts for sales promotion, corporate gifts, fundraising, or educational purposes. Special editions can also be created to specifications. For details, contact the Special Sales Department, Allworth Press, 307 West 36th Street, 11th Floor, New York, NY 10018 or info@ skyhorsepublishing.com.

17 16 15 14 13   5 4 3 2 1

Published by Allworth Press, an imprint of Skyhorse Publishing, Inc. 307 West 36th Street, 11th Floor, New York, NY 10018.

Allworth Press® is a registered trademark of Skyhorse Publishing, Inc.®, a Delaware corporation.

www.allworth.com

Cover and interior design by Mary Belibasakis
Page composition/typography by SR Desktop Services, Ridge, NY

Library of Congress Cataloging-in-Publication Data is available on file
ISBN: 978-1-62153-287-3

Printed in the United States of America

To Dennie

And to Five Decades of Working Together

TABLE OF CONTENTS

PREFACE

Background

Many years ago, after finishing graduate school, I took on my first major work assignment as the executive director of a nonprofit organization. I was very excited. It was my first full-time job, I had won it over several much more experienced candidates, and I felt I was being provided with a career-boosting opportunity.

It wasn't that I lacked nonprofit work experience. I had spent several years working off and on for a nonprofit organization directed by my uncle. It was that experience, my uncle's connections, plus my newly minted doctorate that landed me the job. But I had been doing primarily administrative tasks for my uncle's organization, and though they carried a lot of responsibility, I had never even met his board of trustees. Now, I was going to have to work with a board. I figured I better learn what that was all about. So, I did what many others have done in a similar situation. I signed up for a workshop that promised to teach me what I needed to know about nonprofit boards.

There I was, bright-eyed and energetic, wanting to learn exactly what a board was supposed to do and how it related to my job. I had heard a lot of words associated with boards that I didn't really understand (one—"fiduciary"—I even had to look up in the dictionary). As to the more familiar-sounding words like "governance" and "trusteeship," I didn't really know what they meant in the context of my new organization.

Frankly, I was confused. Some of my friends treated me as though this was going to be "my" organization—I would be the boss. After all, as executive director, I was the head of the organization, they explained. More experienced acquaintances kept asking me about the trustees: what did I know about them and the effectiveness of the board as a whole? Had I spent much time with any of them? Were they philanthropic and good at fundraising?

The answer was, I didn't know. I had met some board members over the course of three formal interviews, but I wasn't acquainted with the others. My friends told me I had better find out because my success would depend, at least in part, on the answer.

I knew the president and liked him. He and I had had an in-depth conversation when I was offered the job. We had haggled some about my salary and benefits, and we had hashed out an agreement fairly quickly. After all, I wanted the job. He said he was acting on behalf and with the authority of the full board. Clearly, if the board had the authority to hire me and set my salary and benefits, they had a lot of power. He also explained—though he said he was sure it would never become an issue—that the board had the legal authority to fire me, and he suggested I read the personnel manual carefully. This was good advice, as it was certainly important for me to get to the bottom of what the relationship was all about.

The workshop was my chance to learn. By the end of the morning, I had gained quite a bit of insight about the kind of organization I was joining. It was called a "nonprofit," not because it couldn't make money—in fact, successful ones did. The point was that unlike a for-profit company, where owners or shareholders could reap a personal profit when the organization made money, there was no such possibility in a nonprofit. No one could personally lay claim on any of the funds that the organization brought in, except, of course, for the staff whose

salaries were already set for the work they were to do or for those providing direct services or products in some other way. No one owned
any part of a nonprofit organization. No one could make money by
selling off the assets. If one reason to be a board member in a for-profit
was to enrich oneself as an owner or shareholder (which board members often were), no such incentive existed in the nonprofit world.

So, if personal enrichment wasn't the goal, what was? If the bottom line wasn't profit, what was it? In fact, it was something elusive
called "public service." Any dollars taken in were to be allocated to
activities serving the mission of the organization (and the associated
costs of realizing that mission). If the money were not spent right
away, it had to be put away in a reserve fund or an endowment fund to
be used later for the public purpose (or provided to another charity).

What was the role of trustees in this kind of structure? Nonprofit
trustees had obligations that were, first and foremost, legal ones. Federal, state, and local governments had granted various benefits and
immunities to nonprofits (like tax deductibility of gifts, exemption
from property taxes, and so on) and they needed to be sure that these
organizations adhered to their public purpose and the law. These
governments could not police every activity and expenditure in
the millions of nonprofits that exist. Rather, they empowered groups
of trustees to do this for them. The trustees were accountable for
making sure that the public was being served and that the relevant
laws were being followed and monies were being spent appropriately.
Indeed, they were *legally* accountable, and in some cases, could be sued
for not doing so. For this reason, trustees were given ultimate authority over everything—finances, policies, even the hiring and firing of
the executive director.

By the time lunch was served, the job was not looking so attractive. The trustees were all-powerful. This hardly sounded like the role
I had coveted.

But after lunch, the picture got a little brighter. I learned that
although the board of a nonprofit organization has legal and fiduciary
(financial) oversight responsibility, it often delegates a huge amount

of this job to a chief executive who serves like the captain of a ship. Once the ship sets sail, the captain takes over, handling day-to-day details. He or she hires the crew (staff), designs the activities (programs), manages the day-to-day finances, and makes sure everything runs properly. The trustees stay ashore, so to speak, entrusting things to the captain. As long as the captain keeps the ship on course and off the rocks and carries cargo and passengers where they are supposed to go, there is no reason for the board to meddle in day-to-day matters. In fact, I learned in a properly governed organization, the board's job was to deal with legal issues, handle policy matters, provide financial oversight, hire the executive director, and most importantly, raise money. So long as the executive director was doing a good job in hiring staff and managing the affairs of the corporation and the board raised enough money, everyone should get along splendidly.

So much for the only professional development workshop I ever paid to attend. Like so many of them, virtually everything I was told was correct. But it was the things not said that day that snagged me for years to come. It was like someone was describing a marriage in which the responsibilities and tasks of the husband and the wife were described to the nth detail, but no one bothered to mention the importance of the *relationship*. Indeed, it turned out that it was the relationship between the board and the executive director—in this book I call it "the magic partnership"—that was the key. When it worked well, almost any problem could be solved. When it didn't, watch out. It was not enough for everyone to do their jobs. It was how the board and executive director functioned *together* that mattered—how they communicated, how they addressed challenges, and how they dealt with shared power and responsibility.

I left the workshop with the idea that if everyone did their jobs well, we would get along splendidly. In my new job, I did run things well; and the board did what it was supposed to do. But we did not "get along splendidly." In fact, after a few years, I decided to leave the organization … only weeks before I probably would have been asked to.

So, what was wrong with the advice I was given? What didn't they tell me? Why didn't everything work out as it was supposed to? That is the subject of this book. In it, I will analyze the nature of the relationship between board and executive director from many points of view in the hope that it will make many people—whether trustees or staff—more effective and show them that there is far more at stake than simply doing one's job well. It is about how to form effective partnerships.

Acknowledgments

I am especially grateful to Marian Godfrey, Naomi Grabel, and Anne Cohn Donnelly for reading an earlier version of this book and making important suggestions. As with most of my writing, Jane Culbert has provided advice on content, style, and offered other editorial suggestions. My editor, Bob Porter at Allworth Press, has worked with me on many projects over the years and once again, his suggestions were invaluable. Thornwell May at Skyhorse Publishing tended to the many details that help an author avoid embarrassing mistakes, keep to a schedule, and produce an impressive looking volume.

Because of the sensitive information in the examples, I do not name specific organizations, and sadly, this means I cannot thank by name the many people whose experiences and personal stories enrich the chapters. Without them, much of the color and fun would have gone out of the book. Hopefully, some will read these pages and recognize themselves and smile knowingly. To all of them, a large collective thank you.

INTRODUCTION

The book, as its title suggests, is about leadership. But unlike some writings that examine the roles, responsibilities, and leadership attributes of a particular individual, this one focuses on the idea of partnership. That is because the specific kind of leadership discussed plays out in a unique setting—that of nonprofit organizations. By their very design, such entities call for a unique power-sharing relationship where specific and distinct roles must be assumed and played by different individuals. Understanding these roles and how the individuals interact is critical to the success of the enterprise.

The book is divided into eighteen chapters. The first chapter describes the different roles and responsibilities of the board and of the executive director in nonprofit organizations in some detail. It also points out why it is so difficult to design hard-and-fast rules defining the relationship. The following chapters each outline a particular challenge in forming an ideal partnership—challenges that can become opportunities for success if each side acknowledges their importance. Some of the chapters treat issues of power sharing; others deal with more mundane questions, like who should speak for the organization in what circumstance, and how board and staff can make efficient use of meeting time. In every chapter, there are one or more case histories to ground the theory in actual practice. There are also a series of questions at the end of each chapter that should help with diagnosing strengths and weaknesses in actual organizations. All the questions are collected together in a concluding appendix that allows for diagnosing board–executive director relationships in a comprehensive way.

The Audience for this Book

Many of the people reading this book will be connected with nonprofit organizations, and it is especially intended to serve their needs with practical and specific examples, as well as diagnostic tools. The questions at the end of each chapter presume such a connection and are focused on looking at strengths and weaknesses within specific institutions.

However, the book is intended for a broader audience, as well. Students who want to learn about the governance and operation of nonprofits will benefit and can use the questions at the end of the chapters as a learning tool. For them, it will be most helpful if they can identify a nonprofit to study, since the issues are far clearer when one can observe them "on the ground."

While the examples and much of the technical information apply to organizations operating according to the laws of the United States, individuals from elsewhere can also benefit from reading the material. In many countries, the model of nonprofit (nongovernmental) organizations is highly developed, and while the laws are different (especially with respect to tax deductibility of gifts), many of the leadership principles are the same.

The book was written both for individuals with little experience with nonprofits and also for those who have served in and around such organizations for a long time. More experienced readers may wish to skim or skip over the material in chapter 1, which provides a fairly basic introduction to nonprofit corporations, their history, and the legal context in which they operate. Others may find the review helpful. Once the book begins to treat specific situations with case history material, experienced readers will also benefit, even if some of the examples simply confirm their own experience.

A Word About Terminology and Examples

In this book, I am consistent in my use of terminology to describe the role of people in nonprofit organizations even though in the real world other descriptors are sometimes used.

- The person who leads the staff I will call the "executive director" even though in some organizations that individual may be referred to as the "president," "chief executive officer (CEO)," or "president and CEO."
- In certain circumstances, I will refer to the head of a for-profit corporation and use the term CEO even though that title is sometimes used for the executive leader in a nonprofit.
- I call members of the governance group or board the "trustees" (in some organizations they are called "directors").
- I call the leader of the board the "president," even though the term "chairman" is sometimes used for this person.

It is important to be able to adjust the terminology to apply to any organization under study and understand that the functions of these individuals remain the same even if the titles used are different.

With respect to examples, I have always found that stories are the best way to illustrate a point, and this book is chock full of them. Some happened to me; others involve people I know.

But because the book deals with sensitive information, I have not been able to use actual names in most cases, and in some, I have had to change essential identifying characteristics or elements of the story. In others, I may have conflated two organizations experiencing similar events and challenges in order to further mask identities and to drive home a point.

Range of Nonprofits

Nonprofit organizations come in all sizes—from tiny, all-volunteer entities operating on a shoestring to complex organizations operating in many cities (and sometimes in many countries) with budgets in the hundreds of millions of dollars. The variety of fields in which they operate is also vast—religion, philanthropy, education, health, human service, domestic and international aid, the environment, and the arts to name just a few—and this means that there is no single set of suggestions that will fit every organization and every situation. Similarly, boards will vary in size (from as few as three people to dozens). Here again, there is no simple guiding principle that will pertain to all of them all of the time.

As a result, what the book tries to do is provide enough examples of the different types of nonprofits and boards so that readers can find themselves or their organizations in many of them. Even when the examples are from a different discipline, or the organization described is larger or smaller than ones the reader has experienced, it will often be possible to adapt the lessons learned and apply them in situations with which the reader is more familiar.

1

GOVERNANCE, MANAGEMENT, AND LEADERSHIP IN NONPROFIT ORGANIZATIONS

It has been almost a hundred years since the United States government laid down a basic legal framework governing nonprofit organizations. The year was 1918, five years after the Sixteenth Amendment to the US Constitution made income tax a permanent fixture in the tax system and gave Congress legal authority to tax incomes of both individuals and corporations. The Revenue Act of 1918 established an important special exception. It allowed organizations involved in certain activities that benefitted the public—functions such as religious, charitable, scientific, public safety, literary, and educational activities—to be exempt from taxation. This one bold stroke enshrined the concept of nongovernmental, public service, and charitable activity in the United States and allowed sectors engaged in such activities to avoid the kind of dependence on direct government subsidy that is characteristic of comparable sectors in other countries throughout the world.

The US Revenue Act of 1954 represented a further development in the story. It set out a modernized tax code that formulated a new set of provisions in section 501(c). In order to enjoy tax-exempt status, a nonprofit corporation had to be organized and conduct business for the benefit of the general public according to certain specified criteria, and it had to fulfill certain requirements as well. It could not have shareholders, it could not have a profit motive, and it had to be free from substantial political activity. In addition to being immune from most forms of federal taxation, nonprofit corporations enjoy another benefit that over the years has become significant—the contributions of anyone (individual or organization) to a tax-exempt, so-called "charitable" nonprofit organization are tax deductible, representing a substantial, indirect government support.[1]

At the same time as federal legislation encouraged more and more nongovernmental charitable and public service activity, a whole body of related state law laid out the requirements of nonprofit corporations that are, in fact, not federal but state-chartered institutions. As these laws evolved, states would often provide tax breaks and exemptions. They would be guided by federal action determining whether corporations met US standards for tax-exempt status. Once the organizations were incorporated and declared tax-exempt, the states would carry out much of the business of regulation of corporate activity (though today the filing of forms is required both by state and federal authorities on a regular basis).

Certainly, one of the most brilliant elements of the design of nonprofit corporations was the concept of unselfish governance—the idea of a governing body, or board, that provides legal and fiduciary oversight without being paid to do so.[2] According to precedent, virtually every nonprofit corporation needs at least three board members who serve as its officers—a president, a treasurer, and a clerk or secretary—all with clear areas of responsibility. These individuals are charged with acting in the public interest (essentially ensuring that the stated mission is being carried out) and monitoring the finances and

---

[1] There are other forms of nonprofit organizations recognized by the Internal Revenue Service where contributions are not tax deductible. These include chambers of commerce, real estate boards, civic leagues, employee associations, and others.

[2] There are certain situations where board members are compensated, but they are rare. A new corporation applying for *tax-exempt* status will often be turned down if it is not clear that board members will be uncompensated.

the operations to be sure laws are being followed. As far as legal matters are concerned, the president certifies various legal documents, the
treasurer certifies financial ones, and the clerk or secretary keeps the
records of the corporation's meetings, at which decisions of the corporation are made. These records are open to review by both the state
and federal governmental units that have jurisdiction. It is important
that each board member can demonstrate a lack of conflict of interest—especially financial interest—in the decisions of the corporation,
which is why the members receive no compensation.

In fact, of course, most boards are a lot larger than three people,
though neither state nor federal law requires them to be so. The business of nonprofit corporations can be complicated and extensive. In
addition, the organization will generally require contributed financial support. Thus, a large board can share the burdens of time, the
need for money, and the other extensive tasks and responsibilities of
governance. In addition, there can be greater incentives in joining a
larger board in the social arena—it can provide an opportunity to
mix and meet others. Being part of a group can be enjoyable, and, in
some cases, can offer opportunities to meet leaders with whom fellow
trustees can do business outside of the corporation's activities. Indeed,
many board members serve in order to make these connections and
advance their own interests, a practice that is legal so long as it does
not cause a conflict-of-interest in terms of corporate governance.[3]

Over the years, board service has come to mean certain things,
and it includes well-documented areas of responsibility:

- Policy making and legal compliance—Drafting the organization's "constitution" (called the "bylaws"), its other policies,
  and ensuring that all applicable laws are being followed.
- Planning—Establishing and approving the activities from
  year-to-year and developing longer-range plans.
- Fundraising—Giving and getting contributions.

---

[3] Cf., Thomas Wolf, *Managing a Nonprofit Organization* (Updated 21st
Century Edition), New York: Free Press, 2012.

- Financial oversight and boundaries—Approving and monitoring a budget, developing all fiscal policies, and commissioning outside examination of the books.
- Hiring and firing—Recruiting, selecting, employing, monitoring, and, if necessary, terminating the employment of an executive director.
- Communication—Providing a communication link with the community promoting the work of the organization.

The notion that a nonprofit organization must be governed by a board accountable to the public and to the government, operating in an unselfish manner, and exercising both fiduciary and legal oversight, has been part of the American system for so long that many are not even aware of its long evolution and what brought it about. It has endured because it works. It is the envy of many other countries throughout the world. And despite occasional lapses, millions of nonprofit organizations have done immeasurable good, because their boards provide insight and a sense of responsibility.

Having reviewed the role of the board in nonprofit organizations, we turn to executive directors, their roles, and their relationships to boards. But here we run into a problem. Quite simply, there is a gap in the legal construct of nonprofit corporations that makes that role of the executive director and the relationship to a board less than clear. The law is explicit about the need for a board, but it is silent on the question of an executive director or chief executive. Indeed, for much of their history, the majority of nonprofit organizations did not have one, and tens of thousands of small nonprofits are still entirely made up of volunteers. And for those that do engage an executive director, the role can vary from someone who is little more than an assistant doing the board's bidding to a world-renowned figure commanding a six or even seven-figure compensation package. What each is supposed to do is technically and legally up to the board that has the responsibility of hiring and firing, as well as delegating powers to the individual.

Thus, while nonprofit governance is enshrined in law and practice, executive directorship is not. Some executive directors are founders of organizations who assemble boards around them and tell trustees what to do—a concept that upends legal requirements and can lead to trouble, as we will see in upcoming chapters. Others are given tremendous authority by their boards with many important functions—including the hiring and firing of a staff, preparation of the annual budget, and strategic planning. Delegating too much authority can be problematic if the board loses sight of its legal obligations. An executive director can be part-time or full-time, compensated or uncompensated, resident or transient. Everything is up to the board.

There are, of course, decades of precedent for how to define the executive director's role, and much of it centers around the concept of executive leadership. While executive directors have no legal function in governance,[4] they are often thought of as the nominal leaders of their organizations. On the one hand, they carry out operational activities, but they also generally represent the organization, either directly or through staff, as it carries out its day-to-day business. An executive director will have overall management responsibility, ensuring the effectiveness of the organization's activities and making sure its financial operation is in order (including preparing and managing the budget). Like the board, executive directors can also delegate, which leads to another of their responsibilities—hiring and managing a staff. Executive directors work with the board on planning, often translating the mission, vision, and goals into concrete programs, actions, and timelines. They often play a major role in fundraising (or have a staff under them that does), and they can spend a good deal of time dealing with members of the community and the constituency, fostering

---

[4] There are exceptions, as when an executive director also serves on the board. However, frequently, the position is designated as "ex officio," and the executive director is excluded from votes that would more commonly be considered the realm of governance trustees.

a positive image of responsiveness for the organization. As we can see, as all these potential tasks are enumerated above, the overlap of executive director and board responsibilities is clear. How to deal with the overlap is not. Efforts to clarify and separate the tasks are often challenging.

Nick had gone through a rough period with his board, and his annual evaluation had confirmed his worst fears. Trustees felt he was crossing the line, getting involved in areas that were their purview. It had begun when Nick had inserted himself into a discussion about the bylaws that the president felt was not in his area of authority. Later, Nick was invited to a planning meeting in which board members were discussing the mission statement, and he vehemently disagreed with a trustee who was a key donor about some suggested wording. Nick, on the other hand, felt that the board was overstepping its authority. He had as a courtesy invited the treasurer to sit in on interviews with candidates for the finance director position, though Nick knew the decision of who to choose should be his. Nick and the treasurer disagreed about who was the strongest candidate and got into a heated argument about who should be hired. In another case, the chair of the marketing committee, a trustee, had persuaded the marketing director to reconfigure his budget so that he could hire an expensive outside consultant. Because the total marketing budget did not change, Nick was not consulted and felt that he had been blindsided when he learned of the action.

In the course of Nick's annual evaluation, he and the board president decided that perhaps making a simple chart outlining board authority and executive director authority would alleviate the problem and have the increased merit of determining whether there were ways to strengthen Nick's job description.

Nick agreed to work with a special ad hoc committee of the board to come up with not only an outline of respective roles and responsibilities, but also actual examples of how each side would act in specific situations.

Nick and the committee met for several weeks. In the end, both agreed that the task was a waste of time. The problems could not be solved by a chart that was either so simplistic as to be meaningless or so detailed that every situation could not possibly be anticipated and captured by an entry in the chart. But what the work had done was to convince all parties of something else: by providing a forum for open communication, many of the problems Nick and the board had experienced evaporated. In fact, since the formation of the committee, there had been no further flare-ups, and it was the concept of communication that became the important lesson.

The relationship between executive directors and their boards in nonprofit organizations is not easy to define with precision. The role that trustees will play may be the clearest to the extent that it emanates from a body of law and decades of precedent, but even it depends on many variables, not the least of which is the individuals who serve. With executive directors, there is no single model that describes the role generically. Executive directors serve at the pleasure of their boards; yet often, they are called upon to lead. They are asked to carry out many tasks, but must defer to the board's authority in doing so.

So, perhaps the best way to proceed is to look at how the relationship plays out in the real world. By looking at actual situations and cases, we can begin to understand the dynamics in depth and find strategies for how to strengthen the relationship into one that ensures mutual respect and success for the individuals involved and the organizations they serve.

Questions

1. Do the trustees understand the nature and obligations of trusteeship in nonprofit corporations? Do they understand their accountability to government and the public?
2. How well are the key areas of board responsibility covered among existing trustees?
3. How is the role of executive director defined in the organization? What are the tasks and responsibilities described in the job description?
4. Where are the areas of overlap in the roles of trustees and executive director? Where are the areas of potential conflict?
5. Have communication systems been established that can defuse potential problems?

2

WHOSE ORGANIZATION?

Two people are sitting in the office of a nonprofit organization. The first is the president of the board. The second is its executive director. Both are asked the same question.

So whose organization is this?

The board president answers first: "I control the board and we have the ultimate power. We set policy. We can change the mission. We can fire the staff. We can even dismantle the organization and put it out of business if we want to. I think the answer to your question is pretty obvious. "

The executive director goes next: "I hate to disagree. Sure, the board can do all the things he mentions. But if the trustees were foolhardy enough to actually follow through, what would they have left? This organization depends on me and my staff. Without us, there is a corporate shell, nothing more."

So who is right—the president or the executive director? Both can exercise a great deal of control over the organization. Both have the power to hobble it. But to thrive, they must work together, remembering that the ultimate "owner" of the nonprofit is the public constituencies it serves. There simply won't be much to preside over if they don't. The power that each wields can be illusory and can quickly slip away.

Let us review just how the power relationship works.

On the board side:

- The legal situation clearly favors the board. Unless the board delegates authority to enter into a contract or expend funds or initiate a program, the executive director has no power to do so. In addition, any legal accountability rests with the board, including accountability for the executive director's actions. The board has the power to change the mission, the direction, even the bylaws and articles of incorporation. The executive director has none of these powers.
- Financial factors favor the board. Financial policies and procedures are approved by the trustees. They approve the budget; they are often the key to raising and giving money to keep the organization afloat. If the organization has an endowment, they control policies with respect to how it is invested and how much can be taken from it (subject to donor restrictions).
- Most important from an executive director's point of view, the board even controls the tenure of the executive director. Trustees establish the contractual terms, including compensation. They determine whether the performance has been adequate; and they have the power to terminate employment.

Why would anyone want to work under such absolute rule? One colleague (I will call him Bill) put it this way: "I finally decided I had had enough, and I changed careers. I left the nonprofit world and decided to start my own for-profit company. For the first time in two decades, I was in complete control. When I woke up in the morning, I didn't have to think about who I needed to consult before making a decision. I just did it. I was my own boss. Everyone worked for me … period. Anyone who feels that way in a nonprofit organization is asking for trouble."

Many people who start nonprofit organizations think their experience will be like Bill's when he established his for-profit business. They use similar words: "I decided to start my own organization." But the pronouns "I" and "my" are problematic. No sooner do the legal forms arrive from the state and federal governments that establish the organization's right to operate than it is clear that more than one person is involved—one signature simply won't do—there needs to be collective accountability. Every nonprofit organization needs multiple officers of the board to sign those forms and the government agencies will recognize those individuals (e.g., president, treasurer, secretary) and their successors as the ones legally responsible for the statements made.

But before despairing, it is important to remember the power of executive directors:

- In many cases, executive directors have deep relationships on the outside—with funders, with program partners, with community leaders, with the media—that are important to the organization. Much goodwill emanates from executive directors. Some critical friends on the outside might be hard-pressed to continue supporting the organization if they felt the executive director's advice had not been followed, or he or she had been ill-treated. Bad press might also ensue, which can be crippling to an organization.
- There are also important relationships that executive directors have with people on the inside—staff and even particular trustees. At worst, an unhappy executive director can lead a mutiny or contribute to such divisiveness that critical staff and trustees might depart.
- The executive director often has a much deeper knowledge than anyone else about the programs and activities, the finances, and even the vision for the future of the organization. When that is lost, it can take months, even years, to regain.

In some cases, it is executive directors who can misjudge the extent of their authority and power.

Bertha started a tremendously successful youth-serving nonprofit organization in the northeast that was considered a national model. She was a pioneer. Her program was innovative. Her ideas were ahead of their time. Bertha was the first of her peers to receive funding from a new federal agency. She was in demand as a public speaker. She gave workshops across the nation. Her board, made up of many friends and associates, were her biggest boosters. "Whatever Bertha wants, Bertha gets," they used to joke.

With time, the organization expanded. Its staff increased, as did the number of its direct service program people, most of whom were independent contractors with no benefits and low pay. Given the success of the venture, they complained about poor compensation, long working hours, and lack of respect from the top. Bertha was off being famous, they said, and did not pay attention to them. When she heard about their complaints, she shrugged them off. "If they don't want to work for us," she said, "there are plenty of others who do."

Over time, the initial board moved on and newer, younger people took their places. Some Bertha knew and others she did not. She didn't pay much attention. After all, the board had always deferred to her. But the carte blanche she had always enjoyed was beginning to dissipate. Some board members did not like her cavalier attitude.

Things came to a head when the independent contractors threatened a work action. Was it a coincidence that that happened to be the day the Internal Revenue Service made formal inquiries about their status as independent contractors (apparently one of the workers had lodged a complaint)? Several trustees, including two attorneys, grew very concerned. They asked Bertha to come to an emergency meeting to discuss the problem.

And that is when Bertha made her fatal mistake. She wrote a letter to the president of the board telling him that she was far too busy to come to such a meeting, and she would take care of the problem herself. The board should not meddle.

One week later, Bertha was out of a job. Her reaction to her firing was characteristic and displayed a great deal of ignorance. "You can't fire me," she said. "This is my organization." But despite her protestations, she had no recourse. The board, exercising its legal and fiduciary oversight function, operated completely within its mandate. They, indeed, had ultimate control.

The fact that a board has ultimate legal power in a disagreement with an executive director is indisputable, as is the fact that the board has the power to fire an executive director (within the constraints established by a contract or a personnel manual, if either exist). But the victory can be pyrrhic and of little value if a treasured and unique executive director decides to walk away, taking along the program, constituents, and even funders.

Stanley had established a similar type of organization to Bertha's. Stanley was African American, educated at elite schools, and had a sterling career ahead of him when he decided he wanted to work with young black kids who had not been given the same opportunities he had. Working in partnership with a local church and using its nonprofit, tax-exempt status to raise money, Stanley's after-school education enrichment program was an instant success. His kids saw their grades and test scores improve dramatically. Parents flocked to the program. So did funders. Press coverage was uniformly positive. Everyone seemed happy.

But the church that hosted the program began to see it as a tremendous opportunity to pursue its own agenda. The board had a vision for how the program could be expanded—which, in turn, would bring in more money, some of which could fund the operating needs of the church. The trustees spoke to Stanley about their plans and the fact that they were planning to bring in someone to help with the expansion. Stanley, not at his most diplomatic, was outraged and let people know it. So were his funders to whom he leaked the news. There was now a standoff, but the church's board stood firm, and, in time, the situation became untenable. Stanley decided the only course was to leave and set up a new nonprofit. While he realized he would leave behind some unspent funds at the church and give up some donated administrative support, he felt the loss was worth it. He took all his students, families, and funders with him— every last one. The church was left with a program that it could no longer afford to run and a lot of embarrassment.

What are the lessons here? Clearly one of them is—to paraphrase Ben Franklin—that boards and executive directors need to hang together if they do not want to hang separately. They need to work on a shared vision and shared goals. They need to communicate their aspirations, concerns, and worries on a regular basis. They need to compromise. The relationship is like a seesaw. The balance of power can shift constantly, with the board sometimes seeming to hold the edge with its legal and fiduciary authority, and the executive director snatching it back with knowledge of the program, loyalty of staff and constituents, and sometimes, crucial funder relationships.

Communication, as we have already noted, is key in any relationship between an executive director and a board. As an experienced board president of a major nonprofit once quipped, "Every year, I make sure I do two things. I go on a vacation with my wife, and I hold a retreat with my board and executive director. Forty years of marriage is evidence that those vacations work. And as for the retreats—well, I haven't had to fire an executive director yet."

Finally, sometimes either the executive director or individual members of the board (or both) simply do not understand their respective roles and the limits of their authority or effectiveness. The use of an outside mediator or consultant to help in such a process can be invaluable, and will be discussed in more depth in chapter 14.

Questions

1. Is there an orientation process for new trustees that introduces them to their role and that of the executive director and staff?

2. Is everyone clear about how legal and fiduciary responsibilities will be properly carried out and what information is needed from the executive director for the board to do its job in this area?

3. Are board members able to convey to the executive director their sense of his or her critically important role in making the organization successful? Do they communicate this in a very public way?

4. Conversely, is the executive director able to acknowledge the important role of the trustees? How often are the words "we" and "our" used instead of "I" and "my" in describing organizational roles and responsibilities?

5. Is the board president someone who is sensitive to the issues surrounding interpersonal partnership? Is he or she someone with sufficient respect and authority to take up the issue with other trustees or the executive director? Are there other trustees who can assist?

6. Are there areas where individual trustees seem to be meddling? How can the executive director be protected in bringing this to the attention of the board and being assured it will be dealt with?

3

WHOSE TRUSTEES?

Acommon complaint of those in nonprofit organizations is the difficulty in finding effective trustees. Once potential candidates are identified, they must be properly vetted and then convinced to serve. Once elected, they need to be oriented and encouraged to carry out their responsibilities. If they are effective, there is the continuing task of retaining them for as long as possible within the constraints of term limits. It is crucial to find people who are willing to take on the many obligations of board service. But this alone is not enough. They must be able to work well with other people, including, very importantly, the executive director.

Making mistakes is costly. It is almost impossible to get rid of trustees who turn out to be ineffective or disruptive. A trustee is a volunteer, after all, not an employee. While there are procedures for dismissal, it is immensely challenging to sack a trustee, except for malfeasance, and it is often awkward even to invite a resignation. True, at the end of a term, trustees need not be reelected, or if they have come to the limit of their terms, they will need to depart in any case without any special action by the board. But sometimes that departure day is a long way off.

Given these realities, recruiting and maintaining a good board should be considered a priority task. And it is one that should be shared, not only among board members, but also with the executive director. To anyone who has read the bylaws of most nonprofit corporations or textbooks describing how governance is supposed to work, this may seem surprising. There are common procedures for choosing trustees, and they generally do not involve executive directors, at least not on paper. The board as a whole nominates and elects the trustees. A nominating committee may coordinate the process. The committee checks for vacancies and then proposes how they will be filled, either through reelection or by finding new candidates. The board relies on the committee to put up a slate on which its members can vote.[5]

In this common process of utilizing a nominating committee, committee members juggle decisions about whether certain trustees whose terms are ending should be reelected, and they determine how many other vacancies can be filled. Trustees who are departing need to be replaced (unless the size of the board is to be reduced), and the individuals who are brought on should bring comparable or enhanced skills, abilities, and financial capacity. While identifying good people to fill vacancies is the nominating committee members' job, presumably they will seek input from other trustees and often

---

[5] There are some boards where "self perpetuation" (that is, a board that nominates and elects its own members) does not or cannot occur. The trustees (or some group of them) may serve *ex officio*, that is, by virtue of their office or position in another organizational entity (e.g., the superintendent of schools or the CEO of the local hospital). In others cases, some other body or individual is responsible for the board appointments (as in the case where each member of a city council may get to appoint one trustee to the organization's board). In these situations, the question of a board nomination and election process is largely mute. But even so, board members and the executive director may have an opportunity to make suggestions where the appointments are discretionary rather than *ex officio,* and they should take every opportunity to do so.

from leaders in the community. If they are wise, they will also ask the executive director for opinions.

Nominating committee members often need and want help and guidance from their executive director. They know that the executive director's ideas matter just as much as those of board members—sometimes more. An executive director will have to work with those selected as trustees. Their actions or nonactions will determine whether there is enough money to operate, whether people in the community admire the organization, and whether the executive director can get the help he or she needs. Trustees even determine whether the executive director will stay or go, and how much he or she will be paid.

Experienced executive directors should be proactive in not leaving the selection of trustees to chance. If there are people who are making life miserable and who need not be reelected, it is important that key members of the nominating committee know who they are. If there are people who aren't pulling their weight, an executive director should give key trustees his or her opinion. And most importantly, if they want good candidates and wish to help build a good trustee team, executive directors can play a major role in finding talented individuals and helping to recruit them or by providing information that could prevent a poor choice from being nominated.

The process of executive director involvement can be subtle. Sometimes their opinions are openly sought. However, not every trustee may be comfortable consulting an executive director in matters of trustee selection. Executive directors are staff and have no authority where the board is concerned. Ultimately, they will be evaluated by the board members who have the power to fire them. The arguments for separation are powerful. There are all too many examples, both from the nonprofit and for-profit worlds, of executive director/CEOs who stacked their boards with friends and colleagues, and when things deteriorated, those individuals didn't call out poor performance and even illegality. Indeed, if there is any question about the executive directors' performance—if they are under probation or doing a poor job—consultation is not recommended.

The nominating committee will make recommendations for new trustees to the full board after canvassing existing board members for suggestions, reviewing candidates' credentials, and subsequently interviewing them.[6] In this process, an executive director may be invited to attend some of the committee meetings, or an individual committee member or two can solicit the executive director's views separately. Indeed, it is behind the scenes that experienced executive directors tend to be most active in the nominating process. It can begin with a frank conversation with the board president, assuming the two have a good relationship. In other situations, the executive director will speak regularly to the chair of the nominating committee or just a committee member. Somehow, the executive director's opinions will be represented—sometimes openly, and sometimes (when selected board members resent the intrusion) through the mouths of surrogates.

What is true of nominees for the board can be even more important when it comes to the nomination of officers. Here especially, the executive director's views matter. Executive directors who cannot work well with their organization's president, treasurer, or other officers are severely handicapped in leading their organizations. A president of the board of trustees is one of the two most important positions in the organization, the other being the executive director. If the two are strong and work well together, things will generally go well. But if one is weak, or if they cannot get along, there can be lots of problems. That is why automatic promotion of vice presidents, which is common in many nonprofits, often does not get you the best person. The bylaws should always give more flexibility.

---

[6] Cf., Thomas Wolf, *Managing a Nonprofit Organization* (Updated 21st Century Edition), op. cit.

Tim had been executive director of a successful nonprofit organization for just over two years when the organization elected a new president, someone Tim did not know well, but who was highly respected in the community. They agreed to meet once a week for the first few weeks of his tenure until they got better acquainted and had shared ideas about key issues and actions that needed to be taken up by the board.

It was during one of these early meetings that the new president asked Tim, "Who is going to be your next board president after me?"

"I have no idea," Tim said. "You were just elected. Presumably, the board has years to decide. Besides, in this organization, the vice president usually becomes president, so we are covered."

"A bad idea," he said. "Is he someone you want to be your next president?"

"No," Tim confided. "He is not particularly strong as a leader, not much of a donor, and hates asking for money. But he has been a loyal volunteer, and people like him and feel he should be rewarded."

"Okay," said the new president. "Let's get started and find you a better one."

The two went over the board list. Tim confided that he didn't see anyone among the officers or the other trustees who he felt was presidential material, and who, just as importantly, would likely accept the position. "Exactly," said the president. "Just what I figured. You confirmed my suspicions. That is why we are talking about it now. We have to go out and find a president. That will take time. We will need to bring that person on to the board, test him or her out on a committee or two, eventually get that individual onto the executive committee, and then into an officer position. That can take years. And what if that person doesn't work out? We will need time to recruit someone else. You should ALWAYS be thinking about your next president and providing your candidate with the proper training to make sure that person succeeds and will be loyal to you in the process."

During the next several years, Tim also learned that assessing trustee performance was one of his most important jobs, one that was not in his job description, but something his president expected him to do. The president taught Tim the trick of using committee assignments as a testing group. "Jana has been complaining about how haphazard our trustee fundraising has been. She says we could raise a lot more money if we were better organized. I have put her on the development committee. Let's see just how good she is at trustee tasks." As it happened, Jana was quite good, and soon found herself an officer of the corporation.

Effective executive directors over time learn to play a role in the process of trustee identification and selection. They also can and should play a role in the selection of officers—especially the president and treasurer with whom they have to work closely. In both of these roles, they may often consult with senior staff, especially the director of development, who may have many insights as to which prospects will bring resources and a willingness to fundraise. Finally, executive directors should assess the performance of trustees and raise the red flag when a trustee's behavior is seriously counter-productive or when contributions (either financial or otherwise or both) are inadequate. While others will have to deal with the situation, executive directors must play a role in identifying problem trustees.

Pete, an executive director, had originally been skeptical of the selection of Barbara as a new trustee. He knew she had run her own business and was wealthy. But he had also heard she was "difficult." Indeed, from her first day on the board, Barbara was critical of how the financial operation was run. People initially paid attention to her comments more than might otherwise be the case because of her success in the business world. She was assigned to the finance committee where many of her recommendations were considered and several put into practice. The director of finance was run ragged and eventually threatened to resign; but Pete talked her out of it and assured her that eventually Barbara would settle down. But things did not improve.

After some sleepless nights, Pete had a frank conversation with the board president and the treasurer. They acknowledged that they were frustrated as well, but they confessed that they were about to approach her for a major gift. Pete agreed to put up with the situation a little longer. A couple of weeks later, after making yet another change in fiscal procedures to satisfy Barbara, the president and treasurer approached her for a capital campaign gift. Her refusal was peremptory and absolute. She would never make a capital campaign gift to the organization. The financial management was sloppy, and anyway, the mission and activities were simply not a priority for her and her husband. The organization could expect her annual fund gift—but that was it.

This was the signal that it was time for action. Pete and his two board members agreed it was time to let Barbara go. Within a couple of weeks, there was a finance committee meeting, and Barbara raised yet another of her objections. Pete cut her off. "No, Barbara. I disagree, and unless the committee overrules me, we are not going to make that change. We have already bent over backwards to address your concerns, and that change would simply be too time-consuming and expensive." No one on the committee said a word, and Barbara got the message. She resigned from the board the next day.

It is true that when it comes to determining the composition of the board, the involvement of the executive director is not legally or explicitly spelled out in corporate governance papers. As a result, that role must be developed carefully in a trusting relationship with key board members. Over time, though, it is in everyone's best interest for an executive director to have trustees and officers with whom he or she can work effectively.

Questions

1. What are the official processes for identifying, nominating, and electing new trustees in the organization? What do the bylaws specify in terms of who is involved in the process?

2. If the appointments to the organization's board are made by another entity or individual, are there ways that existing board members and the executive director can influence those decisions?

3. In the case of self-perpetuating boards, are there formal and open ways that the executive director can be invited to participate in the process of making suggestions and vetting candidates, even if some of the discussions need to be restricted to trustees only?

4. Are there more private ways the executive director can get his or her views taken into account? Is there anyone on the nominating committee who can quietly solicit the executive director's views, with or without attribution?

5. How comfortable are the president and executive director in having frank, private conversations about the performance of current trustees and officers? Can both secure reliable assurances that neither will be quoted without permission?

6. What are the processes by which officers are selected? How active can the executive director be in this process?

4

BUT I HAVE ALWAYS DONE
THAT JOB

There are more than 1.5 million nonprofit organizations in the United States. Astonishingly, almost half have budgets of less than $100,000. Many have no executive director and no paid staff. Even so, the issues they face are important to the topic of partnership described in this book, because as many of these organizations grow, eventually they will need an executive director. And many of them will be ill-prepared for hiring one.

The difficulty of forging a productive working relationship between an organization's first executive director and a board can involve three different kinds of challenges:

- The board must ensure that a volunteer will comfortably step aside and allow the new executive director to do his or her job.
- The board must support the new executive director as he or she gradually professionalizes the work that in the past has been done by volunteers.
- Board members themselves who have primarily acted as volunteers when the organization was small must transition to true governance trustees, shedding old staff-like roles and taking on new responsibilities.

Problem One: Volunteer Executive Directors Who Cannot Let Go

In small, essentially volunteer-driven organizations, board members do many of the jobs that would ordinarily be left to staff. And because someone has to be in charge, a board member generally carries out the functions that in a larger organization would be done by an executive director. Often the system works well, especially if the volunteer is experienced and skilled. But such a structure can only succeed if the organization stays small. When it needs to grow, changes should occur, and the organization must make a transition. But old habits die hard, and people have trouble letting go, especially when they have been successful and they think they know best how certain tasks, including supervisory tasks, should be carried out.

Indeed, the hiring of the first executive director can be fraught with all kinds of problems. Many of these individuals fail because they are undermined by those who have been doing their jobs. Boards must prepare for this moment carefully, thinking deeply about the responsibilities of the new hire, the nature of the supervisory structure and process, and the ways in which a volunteer executive director can effectively transition out of that role. The better the volunteer has been at the job, the more difficult the transition will be.

Consider Nan, the marketing director of one of the largest cultural nonprofits in the world. This is hardly a person one would expect to be involved with the challenge of a first-time executive director. But Nan was one of a group of high-performing, high-achieving women who had decided that sharing experiences informally was not enough; they wanted to create an organization that would address the things they cared about, like networking, communication, and mentoring. "It was partly our attempt to deal in a positive and productive way with the glass ceiling faced by so many women in our field. It was also a way to make sure we didn't let our efforts to get together and talk with one another slip away because we were all so busy."

The new nonprofit corporation was initially supported by membership dues and operated on a shoestring. Clearly, that meant it had to be run entirely by volunteers. Nan described her two years as copresident, during which, as she put it, "I worked my tail off. It was like having a second job. It convinced me that at the very least we would need an administrator, someone who could deal with the considerable amount of paperwork and logistics associated with conferences, awards, and other expanded activities. By the time the individual was hired, our budget had grown to $70,000, and our membership—now international—had grown to 500."

The new administrator was a godsend. She solved many problems and made the organization even more successful. So that meant more growth. At a certain point, the board came to a fork in the road that countless other successful small nonprofit organizations eventually reach. "We realized we needed an executive director. We needed more continuity. Every time the leadership changed, things became precarious. Volunteerism is great, but it can be uneven, especially when people are dealing with high-demand jobs. We needed someone who could give us more time and focus, someone who could help with fundraising and resource development. We needed to maintain visibility and membership and help our board reach consensus, since we all had such strong, independent ideas."

Could anyone fulfill the huge expectations that Nan and her colleagues were placing on this new hire? Could one person magically transform the organization in so many ways?

Nan smiled when she answered that question. "Well, we got our executive director. Her pay was modest, so she turned out not to be as experienced as we would have hoped. And we had been dreaming about what this person would do for so long that our expectations outstripped reality. When that became apparent, several of us did what we so often do in our real jobs: we stepped in to fix the problems. We were reverting to type—playing the roles we played when we were a volunteer organization. By intervening and doing the work ourselves, we undermined the executive director's confidence. Here we were, an organization that took pride in mentoring young women, and we were not practicing what we preached."

Today, Nan no longer is involved with the organization she helped to found. "I was the right person for the entrepreneurial phase, but now the organization has much more appropriate people serving on the board, people who know how to be board members and let the executive director do the tasks she was hired to do."

Nan and her colleagues learned an important lesson. The moment at which a nonprofit organization hires its first executive director is a critical time when lots can go wrong. The move has ramifications that go well beyond issues of growth and efficiency. For trustees, especially, roles will have to change. The balance between doing and overseeing—between management and governance—shifts radically. For many trustees who have been happy with their volunteer administrative responsibilities, the shift is a shock and not always a happy one.

Problem Two: Professionalizing the Staff

The second challenge facing an organization's first executive director is the need to shift jobs from community volunteer positions to paid ones. Volunteers who have done those tasks well can resent being replaced, especially when they believe the individual does not have the skill, commitment, or loyalty that they themselves brought to the job. It is hard enough for board members to stand back and support the executive director when they themselves can do the work. But it is especially frustrating when individuals who they know have done a wonderful job in the past—often people from the community who have given much time and effort—come to them and complain.

Margaret is a talented woman who, a number of years ago, conducted a feasibility study for a new school as part of an assignment for a graduate course in nonprofit administration. Originally, her work was purely academic, but over time, Margaret got so excited about the results that she went ahead and founded the institution she had conceived of in her project. Her original study indicated that there was a strong demand for the school and the organization turned out to be an instant winner. Despite strong demand, money was tight at the beginning, and Margaret had to rely on volunteers for many administrative tasks. Happily, she found a group of senior citizens, some former teachers, who agreed to help out, giving free time in various programmatic or administrative capacities. The school provided new excitement in their lives, and they were delighted with the organization and with Margaret.

At a certain point, Margaret realized she could no longer serve both as board president and an unpaid director. It was simply taking too great a toll on her personal life. So, she convinced the board that what was needed was an executive director, a job she herself was not interested in. The hiring of this individual brought welcome relief, and Margaret was more than happy to turn over the reins. Her enthusiasm was initially shared by the board, whose members felt that they had picked a talented individual who was popular with students, teachers, and parents.

Soon, however, there was a crisis. The executive director shifted many of the jobs that volunteers had been doing to paid staff. To compound the problem, some of the affected volunteers were good friends of board members, and the changes came as a complete surprise to the trustees. The reaction was instantaneous. Several members of the board resigned, and others had to step in and quell the fires of resentment so the executive director could do her job. "She doesn't understand," said one of the board members about the executive director. "Our volunteers did it differently and so much better. This is such a waste of money." More experienced trustees, including Margaret, realized that leaving space for a new executive director to do things in a different way (even if it meant some mistakes and inefficiencies) was crucial. But the road was bumpy, and there were many hard feelings.

Can a transition from volunteers to paid staff be handled differently and more effectively? Yes, but it once again involves teamwork between an executive director and a board. Together, they can develop a transition plan rather than relying on an executive director's unilateral approach. In addition to not catching the board off guard, an executive director can deflect some of the blame, and the board can share in the responsibility. Sometimes, an executive director can reason that with many volunteers close to board members or even serving on the board themselves, there likely will be resistance and delay in implementing a professionalization plan. But in this instance, a skilled leader, working closely and quietly with selected board members, can garner support for change and save a great deal of time and unhappiness, often preventing continuing suspicion of motives from key members of the board.

Problem Three: Learning How to Be Trustees

The final problem that small nonprofits face when they grow concerns the changing nature of trustee responsibility. Many boards begin as a small circle of acquaintances, often grouped around a founder-director, either volunteer or paid. All too often, the board role has been inadequately described, and some people take it on, believing that it is essentially honorific, or that it takes the form of a volunteer task or two. But organizational success can gradually change the requirements of trusteeship: fundraising, policy making, fiduciary oversight, and a host of other responsibilities soon become part of the portfolio, and for some, it can look like an overwhelming job, one they never signed up for. In this case, "I have always done that job" can mean "I have always done the job of trusteeship my way … and I do not intend to do it any other way."

Myron started a small nonprofit organization with the help of some good friends who turned out to be willing key donors. His contributors, one of whom ran a foundation and another of whom held national office, loved both Myron and his concept, and they wanted to give him enough money so that he could pay himself a salary and serve as an executive director right from the start of his new organization. But all were busy people, and they made it clear they would not want to serve on a board. Rather, they encouraged Myron to go out and find others to do so. He assembled another small group of friends quickly, telling them there wasn't much they had to do—he had things in hand.

For Myron, the problem was too much success, too soon. It wasn't long before his organization grew to the point where he needed his trustees to act more like a board. His original donors continued to give money, but it was not nearly enough. He needed his board to give and get money, to network and find other trustees, and to help him develop an organizational structure and strategic plan. He wanted someone who understood financial management to help him set up an accounting system. He needed marketing expertise. But none of that had been part of the original deal, and not surprisingly, nothing much happened.

Myron was fortunate in that his board president was an individual experienced in nonprofit trusteeship. Over time, he mentored other board members about the responsibilities of trusteeship, sharing books and articles on the subject. In some cases, individual board members rose to the occasion, and in others, people saw the handwriting on the wall and resigned. Together with Myron, the two developed a simple growth plan, laying out everyone's responsibilities. The trustees were enthusiastic, but there were still some who remained inactive and unwilling to step down. Rather than make waves, the president waited until their terms were up, thanked them, and made sure they were not reelected for subsequent terms.

So many problems can be avoided if the responsibilities of trusteeship are spelled out from the beginning of a recruitment process. This is as true for a tiny organization as for a large one, for as we have seen, small, successful organizations have a tendency to grow. Most importantly, it is as necessary for an executive director to understand these responsibilities as it is for the trustees. The executive director is often the one in a small organization who does the recruiting, and the inability to lay out board responsibilities clearly and unambiguously will reap unhappy consequences down the road.

Questions

1. Is the organization too small for an executive director at this time? What key indicators would signal that one is needed?
2. What steps must take place for a first-time executive director to be successful? How can an existing volunteer leader be helpful without being intrusive, while ultimately stepping aside?
3. What support will the board provide to help an executive director professionalize the staff of a growing organization, replacing volunteers with paid staff?
4. How fully cognizant are the trustees of their governance responsibilities? Has organizational growth shifted their roles?

Who is primarily responsible for reeducating them about what will be required of them in the future?

5. Is there a glide path for volunteers (including board members) who are not comfortable with change, helping them transition to new roles?

6. What are the main talking points as trustees and the executive director talk to board prospects about governance responsibilities in the organization?

5

SO YOU WANT MY ADVICE . . .

There is an old adage that a nonprofit organization needs four things from its board, each of which starts with "w":

- It needs *wealth*—people who will give money.
- It needs *workers*—people who will give time and effort.
- It needs *worriers*—people who will give attention to things like finances and legal requirements.
- Finally, a board needs *wisdom*—people who will give sage advice.

On a very good board, most trustees have one of the four "w's," and the board as a whole is balanced with all these strengths. If one is missing, there can be problems, especially if the board is dominated by a single category. One might think a board consisting only of wealthy, generous individuals would be ideal; but unless other requirements of good governance are covered, the organization is vulnerable.

Many boards are overrepresented by people who are there primarily for their knowledge or expertise—the advice-givers who bring the fourth "w"—wisdom. These people can have great value. For example, it is not unusual for an executive director to look to board members for advice on business questions, personnel matters, technology, and other specialized areas. But each of these areas of wisdom can come with a downside if the individuals do not have a larger sense of the realities in which nonprofit organizations operate. Business people may bring advice from their experiences in very large for-profit corporations, where a marketing budget is a hundred times larger than the budget of the entire nonprofit. Conversely, they may offer personnel advice based on an idealized notion of nonprofits, assuming that therapy and love is better than dealing forthrightly with staff incompetence or maliciousness. A technology expert may be more enamored of the latest gadgets and push the organization toward unproven hardware and software.

Lopsided board composition favoring advice-givers often occurs when organizations are young—when trustees may be hard to come by, and recruitment depends almost entirely on triggering interest in what the organization is doing. Later, as organizations grow and as more people of substance, wealth, and trustee experience are attracted to a board because of the organization's growing impact on the community, organizations can become more selective in who they recruit, looking for those who bring other attributes.

But even in cases of mature organizations, there are times when the balance shifts too far toward the so-called "wise." The allure of "experts" may be hard to pass up, especially when they come with an impressive or even world-renowned resume. One historical organization was able to entice a couple of Pulitzer Prize-winning writers; a symphony orchestra recruited several world-famous musicians with household names; a university could not pass up two Nobel laureates, one of whom had graduated from the institution, and the other who served on the faculty. There would have been nothing wrong with having such people on the respective boards had they been truly prepared to fulfill their board service. But in each case, the individuals were too busy to serve conscientiously and tried to make up for it by offering off-the-cuff advice when they were around, often not in their areas of expertise. Compounding the problem, these were individuals accustomed to having their opinions treated as gospel, and they did not take well to having advice ignored. There might well be other places that these organizations could have placed such stars in order to capture their fame and their knowledge, without adding the governance function to their responsibilities.[7] But the board of trustees was not the place.

Another tricky situation can occur when an organization needs board members with a lot of expertise because the activities of the organization are quite technical or esoteric, and people without specialized knowledge might have difficulty understanding the issues involved. The danger here is that there is no assurance that the individuals serving on the board understand what it means to be a trustee of a nonprofit organization and may be unfamiliar and uninterested in the normal expectations of trusteeship.

So, how does this situation of so-called "wise" trustees impact an executive director? The following case study provides an illustration.

Linda was executive director of what one of her peers described as "a real hot-shot nonprofit." Its programs centered on new media. A local magazine described her board as "hip—the kinds of people you would go to a party to meet." Her trustees consisted of technology and media experts who were young, smart, opinionated, successful, and did not suffer fools gladly. "What I wouldn't give to be at one of their board meetings," a young developer of mobile apps said to a colleague.

If he had only known! Linda's board was smart—no question about it. But they could never seem to decide anything. They were too busy critiquing Linda—and each other—and giving advice. Every time a major decision had to be made, Linda prepared material in advance—often in great detail and

---

[7] Some organizations not only have a governing board, but also have another group that is largely advisory in nature. In some organizations, these are called the "Overseers." Others have "Visiting Committees" of experts to advise them. Some simply have Advisory Boards.

with lots of back-up research. Sometimes, consultants were hired to provide additional context and recommendations. Linda made sure board members were interviewed in these cases. But invariably, when the full board came together to discuss a recommended action, one group of trustees would point out that the research had not been comprehensive enough, another would recommend a different approach, and a third would say that the whole initiative was misguided because it was investing in the wrong technology. Linda and her staff would go back to the drawing board, consult with committees, and send out reports for review and comment. But it seemed that each time important ideas would come up for a vote, they would be tabled, pending just one more piece of information or consultation.

Clearly, one of the problems was that Linda's board included many trustees for whom this was their first experience with a nonprofit organization. Working in a field where being smarter than the next guy was considered an asset, they had little experience with the importance of compromise and of group decision making. They seemed to be unaware of how their behavior was putting the organization at risk, and making Linda wonder about whether she ought to be looking for another job.

Problems came to a head when the organization was encouraged to apply for a major, new, multiyear, seven-figure grant from a media company. To secure the funds, Linda had to submit a plan for the use of the money and identify new partnerships that could extend the impact of the work. It looked like her organization was a shoo-in for the money. She and her staff had the expertise, knowledge, and organizational infrastructure to deliver. The problem was the board. They simply were second-guessing everything and were unwilling to grant approval until Linda got things just right, even though the trustees were not in agreement among themselves about what "just right" meant. After six months, the funding source was getting impatient. Deadlines were being missed. There was a real possibility that the funding would fall through.

Why wasn't the partnership between board and staff working? There were a lot of smart people sitting around the table. Why, with all that brainpower, was it so difficult to come up with a decision?

Actually, the brainpower can be part of the problem if it all is of the same kind and duplicates the expertise that the executive director and the staff already have. Partnerships, like good marriages, often work best when the partners bring complementary strengths and differing perspectives. In a nonprofit organization, this is even more important, since the roles of trustees and staff members need to be clearly differentiated. In the case presented above, one of the four "w's" (wisdom) was present. But the lack of the others—in this case, especially the worriers who should have sent up a red flag about the impact of the dysfunctionality on long-term funding prospects—was hampering the organization in serious ways.

In many organizations, several board members have been invited to serve because of their knowledge. Like the staff, they are experts in the field. They are not there for fundraising, or fiduciary oversight, or for carrying the organization's message to the community, or for any of the host of other functions normally associated with trusteeship. They have been invited to provide expertise and advice—period. So in a sense, their reluctance to approve things that they feel are not truly "ready" for approval may seem appropriate. In Linda's case, the organization, with Linda's full support, had gone after these individuals on the misguided assumption that adding to the pool of technical expertise was just what was needed. Is it any wonder that these trustees were prepared to roll up their sleeves and carry out the tasks the staff was hired to do? In a sense, each trustee saw his or her role as serving as a shadow executive director.

The same problem can be found in organizations that have a dedicated stream of funding that makes conventional fundraising unnecessary. An organization supported by membership dues is one example. Another is an organization in which a founder has given a large endowment sufficient to operate the institution; in still another, a group of foundations may provide the wherewithal for the organization to operate without the need for trustees to focus on fundraising. If board members have neither to give nor get money, their tendency is to give advice instead, and that advice can often shift from an appropriate oversight function to inappropriate program design and implementation ideas.

What steps did Linda's organization take to solve the problem of too many technology experts?

The first solution was the most obvious. Change the composition of the board. In Linda's case, it did not take a lot of changes, but as vacancies arose, she and the board president vetted and later filled the vacancies with individuals whose knowledge and experience had less to do with technology and media and more to do with trusteeship and the importance of the support role of the board. Linda privately called these new recruits her "grown-ups," individuals who could say in a meeting: "These are all good ideas, but we also have a strong staff, and we must move things along. A lot of good work has been done, and I am sure Linda and her staff will take all the discussion today into consideration once they begin the final design and implementation of the program."

The second important step was to spend time defining more clearly the roles and responsibilities of trustees and differentiating those roles from those of the staff. It was Linda's grown-ups who suggested the board go through an exercise where they brought in a trainer to help board and staff together work out their respective roles. As things became clearer, some of the original techno-wizards resigned from the board; this was not for them. Others agreed to serve on a technical advisory committee that could get into the detail of program development, but not waste precious board time arguing the niceties of technical options.

Finally, Linda and her board president learned an important principle of governance and decision making—never leave important decisions to chance. After materials were sent out prior to board meetings, Linda and the board president made calls to key board members asking if they were comfortable with the direction of the meeting and the content of the action items. They made sure that these individuals were prepared to support the action items and often asked whether specific board members would make or second the motion for adoption. In some cases, it was agreed that certain modifications were acceptable, but the key was that there would be no delays in moving ahead.

"I continued to get advice," said Linda, "and now I actually welcome it. Because now it isn't keeping us from doing the work we need to do."

Questions

1. How well are the four "w's" (wealth, workers, worriers, and wisdom) represented on the board? Where are the gaps?

2. Have the president and the executive director had an opportunity to speak frankly about getting more balance on the board, and is there a mechanism for doing so?

3. Are board members who are knowledgeable about programs and activities too involved in day-to-day decisions? Is there a mechanism by which the executive director can safely and privately raise concerns about the problem?

4. Is there an experienced and skilled president (or other trustee) who can help remind those who are acting as shadow staff that this is not an appropriate trustee role?

5. Is there a committee structure that allows trustees who have in-depth knowledge and interest about an area to have an opportunity to express their views and make suggestions? If so, is it made clear to them that their role is advisory only?

6. Are there ways that important decisions can be vetted early, prior to the time they are voted on by the full board, to ensure that they will not be held up?

6

PICKING A WINNER
(WITH A LITTLE HELP)

How should a board identify and recruit an ideal candidate to be executive director, someone who will inspire, lead, and work well with trustees, staff, and the community? That is a question that numerous textbooks try to answer. Many focus on the importance of succession planning so that there is a set of procedures in place when the incumbent has to be replaced. Because such moments can be unanticipated—a sudden resignation, a death, or even a rapid termination—it is best to have thought about the steps that will be taken beforehand, rather than having to develop them in a more time-pressured moment. In addition to how the position will be filled by a permanent hire, the plan must address issues of interim management and be sure the necessary talent is available—on the staff, the board, or elsewhere—to take on the important temporary role.

But there is another question about succession that is less common: how might a retiring executive director assist in the process? And why should that help sometimes be desirable?

It is important to begin the discussion by acknowledging that, in many instances, the last thing a board wants is the involvement of an outgoing executive director. In many cases, the departure is acrimonious; in others, the particular attitudes of the incumbent will work against changes the board believes are necessary. Sometimes, the executive director is leaving with little advance notice, and board members are less than thrilled about trying to involve an individual who they believe cares so little about the health of the organization (even if this is unfair, the sour attitude of board members must be taken into account in such a delicate situation).

But there are instances where an executive director's opinion and help can be invaluable. To understand when and why, it is necessary to take a step back and explore some of the unique challenges of staff leadership in nonprofit organizations.

Several years ago, the Pew Charitable Trusts in Philadelphia commissioned an internal study of leading nonprofit organizations in the arts field. They hired a team of consultants to help identify the organizations (as nominated by peers and professionals from other foundations), and subsequently determine the characteristics that made them successful.

Not surprisingly, one consistent finding was that all the organizations were led by executive directors who were highly effective and well-respected people. They knew how to lead, they were curious, they thought about the future, they made themselves available to their key supporters, and they got on well with their boards. The obvious question was: had these organizations been uncannily lucky, or was there some knack to identifying such talent?

Unfortunately, it turned out that there was no magic formula, and in many cases, organizations claimed they had just been lucky. However, one board president, a CEO of a Fortune 100 company, was extremely forthcoming about the dynamics of the process in nonprofit organizations.

Like many of his fellow trustees who worked in large for-profit corporations, the president explained that he spent much of his day in a business environment that nurtured executive talent and identified prospective leaders. If something were to happen to him, a handful of individuals from within his company could replace him the next day. These individuals had been groomed for his job, and one or another of them might well be selected to succeed him at some time in the future. They had lived the corporate culture. They knew the operation. They had been tested. They were known by the board, staff, and public. If one of them were selected, the company could probably continue on without missing a beat. Even in considering individuals from outside the company, those who would make the choice knew they were already dealing with a deep talent pool.

In nonprofits, though, there is rarely the luxury of nurturing leaders just below the top level. How many of the individuals who report to an executive director have been trained for the executive director's job? Not many. It is simply too expensive for most nonprofits to have executives-in-waiting, and it is not part of the culture as it is in large for-profit corporations. It is true that nonprofit organizations sometimes promote from within, and sometimes with great success. But often, it is because they cannot attract or pay for the kind of leader they really wish they could have, and the track record is uneven at best.

For those nonprofits in a position to have pretty much who they want, what do they do when their executive director departs? Typically, they go out and search for another one—often poaching in the territory of another nonprofit where someone looks to have the right portfolio of experience. But it is experience developed elsewhere. It is always a risk. Boards may do all they can to ensure that the individuals will succeed, but there will always be a learning curve and productivity time lost in the orientation process. And there is always the risk that trustees, most of whom have little to no working expertise in the nonprofit's field, will select the wrong person whose knowledge and chemistry simply doesn't mesh easily. Search firms can help alleviate some of the problems, and they increasingly play a major role. But the challenges remain.

Many nonprofit organizations have an asset that is underutilized in the search process and that can provide much of the expertise and support lacking. That asset is the outgoing executive director. This is a person who generally knows a great deal about the organization, how it operates, and how senior staff must relate to the community and various constituencies. The individual also may be very familiar with the field and the talent pool within it. Once candidates are identified, the outgoing executive director can be the organization's best sales-man when a desired candidate starts getting serious about the job (or can help avoid disasters by ensuring that candidates do not take the helm with false and exaggerated expectations).

Certainly, there are many instances when executive directors should not be involved in any way in helping to find their replacements. Some are moving on because they have been asked to leave or are departing under a cloud. Some have spawned ill will in the process of resigning and have lost the trust and admiration of their boards. Oth-ers go so quickly that they have no interest or capacity to help their old organizations while they are dealing with challenging relocation issues and a new job that is demanding time on site even before it begins.

But in other cases, the executive director can be a critical asset in a search and replace process. What are the things an outgoing executive director can bring to the process of leadership transition?

- One valuable asset is time—giving ample notice so that the process need not be rushed. Especially in the case of a retirement, an out-going executive director may have the luxury of planning plenty of time between notifying the board of the decision to retire and actually departing.
- Another is providing some flexibility in a departure date, depending on how long the process of naming a successor actually takes. It is important, though, that the board must know there is a certain date after which the executive director will leave. The board cannot be lulled into the mistaken notion that ample notice means there is no urgency.
- The third form of assistance the outgoing incumbent can provide is a carefully designed interim administrative structure, with a poten-tial temporary executive director who can provide leadership if the

board's search extends beyond the incumbent's tenure. Ultimately, it will be up to the board to decide what will work best and who will be in charge. But having suggestions from someone who knows how the everyday business of the corporation is conducted can be helpful.

- Fourth, the executive director can provide various kinds of advice. He or she can sketch out for the board various alternative visions for the future of the organization and might suggest names of candidates who could be appropriate for each scenario. If the future model is growth and expansion into new areas, that may call for one form of leadership. If it is consolidation, a different constellation of skills might be best.

- Fifth, once candidates are identified, the board may wish to have the executive director's candid assessment of their abilities, should he or she be familiar with the individuals.

- Finally, the incumbent should be available to talk to candidates frankly, honestly, and confidentially about the situation they are walking into. Some boards worry that there are too many negatives that could scare away prospects. But better to get them out in the open before someone is hired, than to have things discovered later.

With all these forms of assistance, the departing executive director needs to leave enough space for the board to make the decision without interference and undue influence. For this reason, it is probably not a good idea for the individual to serve on a search committee or have some official role in voting on the replacement. Actual or perceived biases could weaken the integrity of the process. And should the board decide not to involve the executive director in the process in any way, the incumbent must agree not to try to impose his or her opinions. When a search consultant or search firm is used, there may be even less reason to involve the incumbent in substantive ways. But people involved with search processes coming in from the outside will often rely on the outgoing executive director to make their jobs easier.

Terrell was a retiring executive director who had led his organization for two decades. He was well-known in his field and beloved by his community. Knowing the board would need ample time to replace him, Terrell let it be known six months in advance he would be stepping down. Terrell believed strongly that much as he believed he knew the best way forward for his organization and was tempted to lead another strategic planning process, the worst thing he could do was to impose that vision on others. At the final board retreat of his tenure, a month after he announced his resignation, he spoke of a number of directions he hoped the organization might consider over the next decade—directions that could influence the kind of executive director the board was looking for. Later, he provided the board president (confidentially) with a list of people he felt might be excellent candidates. One of these was his deputy director.

A search committee of the board handled the process from there. All of Terrell's candidates were contacted and others were also considered—the position had been posted and advertised and resumés came flooding in. Four individuals not on Terrell's list contacted him about the position. With the consent of his board president, he talked to them about the job and the organization, and ultimately only one decided to apply. A first round of phone interviews by members of the board search committee was followed by a narrowing of the field. At this point, four candidates were invited to come for visits. Each was given time with Terrell. Terrell was frank about what he saw as the challenges and the opportunities. On the basis of the conversations, another candidate withdrew.

It was at this point that Terrell was most tempted to intervene. As he explained later, "I had behaved well. I did what I was asked and laid back when not asked. But of the three candidates,

I felt one was totally unsuitable, one was okay, and one was a superstar. I also felt some of the criteria the search committee was using were just plain wrong and would lead to the unsuitable candidate. But no one asked me what I thought. I came close to calling search committee members several times, but just kept telling myself, 'You have to let go.'"

In the end, Terrell's "superstar" was not hired. But he could console himself that his "unsuitable" candidate also did not get the job. And, looking back five years later, Terrell acknowledged: "You know, they probably picked the right person."

There is one other important detail to insist upon when an executive director helps in the process of selecting his or her successor. The incumbent must commit to supporting the board's choice publicly once the decision is made. There can be no second-guessing the decision, especially when this individual is talking to those in the broader community who may be looking for signs from the former leader. Being positive and upbeat (or at least supporting the integrity of the selection process) may be the greatest help the outgoing executive director can provide, and though it may sometimes be challenging, as it was initially in Terrell's case, it will greatly aid in a smooth and effective transition.

Questions

1. How well-equipped is the board to identify and recruit a new executive director? Is there a succession plan in place?

2. Are there any staff members who could conceivably be future executive directors in the organization? Are there any processes in place to nurture them for possible future leadership?

3. Has the outgoing executive director provided a reasonable amount of notice? If not, can anything be done to encourage more time before his or her departure?

4. Has a proper interim administrative structure been set up to ensure appropriate leadership during a possible transitional period between an outgoing and incoming executive director?

5. Is it appropriate to ask the outgoing executive director for assistance in the search for his or her successor? Is the relationship such that the board feels comfortable making the request?

6. If yes, in what ways can the outgoing executive director assist in the identification of a successor? Providing a vision of the future? Identifying desired qualities needed in a successor? Providing a list of actual candidates? Vetting candidates? Speaking confidentially and honestly to candidates about the position?

7

TURNING ON THE SPIGOT

Can an executive director get a board to give more money? It is an age-old question, one that comes up repeatedly in fundraising workshops when executive directors share their most frustrating challenges. This chapter offers tips on how an effective (and sometimes fairly invisible) partnership between an executive director and a board member or two can entice certain trustees to make their very first contributions and others, who are already giving, to give more.

Let's start with the basics. First, it is a fundamental tenet of nonprofit governance that giving money is a primary responsibility of a board member. There are exceptions, of course. Some boards include *ex officio* members, such as a school superintendent or a mayor, who are there by virtue of their jobs and are not expected to contribute money. Other boards have honorary members or those appointed by public officials according to statute who are not required to contribute. Still others, such as national service organizations that are supported largely through membership, have boards composed almost exclusively of working professional members, and there is no expectation that they give money.

But setting these cases aside, the basic rule is that board members are expected, and in some cases, required to give money. Whether, where, and how the expectation or requirement is stated and how it is enforced is often a central element in diagnosing problems. More often than not, if something is written down at all, it is not an official policy of the organization, voted by the trustees, and therefore enforceable. And even when the policy has official standing, as in the bylaws or the minutes of meetings in which the policy was voted, enforcement is something else entirely. While technically it is the board's job to police its own giving, there are many cases in which it can fall down on the job.

Yet, if not the board, then who? It is awkward for the executive director to step in and remind trustees of their obligations. The executive director works for the trustees and is evaluated by them and can be fired by them. Telling trustees that they are failing in their obligations is not an enticing prospect under any circumstances, and certainly not when your own job is dependent on their good will. Forcing the executive director into the role of board-giving enforcer is simply unfair. And it is also impractical, since most executive directors will figure out ways to avoid taking up the issue with problem trustees.

But there are ways in which executive directors can orchestrate enforcement. They have the information on giving, and often they have the "script" of what needs to be said. What they need is a mouthpiece, and a trusted board member can often fill this role with some help and coaching.

Tom was in his midtwenties and still in graduate school when he was invited to serve on his first board. The board he ended up joining governed a small, separately incorporated, local chapter of a national nonprofit coalition. His mother had served on the national board with distinction for many years, and she had been quite a colorful and beloved member. When one of the chapters learned that her son lived in the area, a trustee immediately asked him to join the local board. After receiving the invitation, he called his mother to ask whether it was appropriate to accept, given his limited time availability and even more limited trustee experience. She said. "You should do it. I have heard they need you."

Once Tom attended his first board meeting, he realized his mother had not been exaggerating; he might be of some assistance to a hard-working executive director who had to struggle with a rather inactive board. Tom met with her privately to learn about the organization and received an earful of complaints about problems, especially in the financial area. Despite the impressive list of board members and the obvious wealth of some of them, the organization's finances were in a shambles. And it was clear why. The trustees were not giving much money—indeed, some gave nothing at all.

"Give, Get, or Get Off." That much, at least, Tom had learned from his parents, and he had already put aside money to contribute. He accepted the board assignment, knowing that trustees need to donate, they need to raise money, and if they don't do these things, they need to get off the board and make room for others who will. He remembered the argument. The board should be the first line of support. They need to set the standard of giving, and then they must go out and raise more. Well, it certainly wasn't happening in this organization.

What to do? Tom had no idea. The executive director spoke confidentially and frankly to him. "My dilemma," she said, "is that I am the wrong one to complain. I can't tell the board members they should be giving more. It has to come from the board itself. But no one is willing to tackle the issue, not even the president who, compared to the others, is rather generous. I need help from someone, and if you are willing, I can coach you on what to say."

Tom and the executive director waited for an appropriate opportunity to inject the issue into a board discussion in a natural and unforced way. That opportunity was a discussion of the budget for the coming year. There was much hand-wringing about how difficult it was going to be to balance the budget, given how little money had come in. Tom raised his hand. "How much of the individual contributions are coming from the trustees?"

The question was not spontaneous. It had been planted by prior agreement between Tom and the executive director, so an answer was immediately forthcoming by her: it was a paltry sum that trustees contributed. "My," Tom said (again well-prepared). "That's a very small number. How many of us are giving?" When told that only about half the trustees were donors, Tom tried to look shocked. "Well, I know I am the youngest one here, and I should probably defer to others. But people I respect a lot have told me that in nonprofit organizations, all trustees should be contributing something."

After an awkward silence, the meeting moved on. But Tom wouldn't leave it there. The next day, he wrote a letter to his fellow trustees, saying that he had rechecked with a friend who worked at a foundation, and he had been informed that most foundations would not consider a grant application from an organization unless there were 100 percent trustee participation in giving. "So let's set ourselves a modest goal this year of 100 percent participation by the trustees in giving, and a $10,000 total from the board. Give what you can. But since there are twenty-five of us, you can figure out what we need to average per gift."

Gifts started coming in—some a lot larger than the $400 average that was needed. One trustee sent $500 and wondered whether she should resign, given that she couldn't afford what she said was "the full $4,000 average gift." Clearly, her math skills were not very good, and Tom assured her that, as she had in fact exceeded the average, there was no need to resign. After a week, Tom called those he had not heard from, and in one case, went to someone's home in the evening to pick up the check. In the end, the money taken in was almost double what he had set out to raise. In addition, there were three resignations from the board (which Tom and the executive director privately celebrated), and there was 100 percent giving from the rest. The organization then enacted a policy stating that for trustees, failure to make a cash gift in any year constituted an automatic resignation from the board.

Here was a case where the magic partnership worked to a tee. The executive director had a problem with trustee giving that only a board member could help solve. Working together, trustee and executive director got results that were better than either had expected.

Once a board achieves a 100 percent trustee-giving track record, it should officially memorialize the policy and the expectation. This can be done through an official vote at a board meeting, and the policy then can be shared with all prospective trustees and any existing trustees who may not be aware of it. In some cases, the board may also establish a minimum giving level for trustees, though this can be controversial and counterproductive. Some people believe that setting the level too high discourages people from serving on the board. Others say setting it too low discourages wealthy people from giving at higher levels. In many cases, experts feel it is best to set goals for the board as a whole and increase these goals each year as the levels are met or exceeded. Each organization must decide for itself whether a minimum giving level will in the end be good for board fundraising.

One thing is certain, however: getting people to give something may be less of a problem than getting those with the wherewithal to give at a level more commensurate with their capacity. This is common in organizations that have been around a long time and have boards with slow turnover. Standards of giving established early in the organization's history get reinforced as new trustees come onto the board. The level of board giving does not grow, and modest contributions become part of the corporate culture. An executive director can hint at the problem by talking about other similar organizations that get higher board gifts and say how wonderful it would be if the trustee line in the fundraising budget could be increased. But all too often, there will be few trustees taking the bait. Once again, a quiet partnership can be the way to go.

Sarah was an executive director who felt frustrated that nothing she could say would change the situation. Her board was simply not giving enough money. After one especially deflating board meeting, she received a surprise call from a trustee. "Look," he said, "I get your problem—actually, I should say, our problem. We have a board of skinflints, and someone has to light a fire under these deadbeats. I think I see a way to do it, but I will need your help. I inherited some money this year, and I was going to give it to the organization anyway. Tell you what I will do. I will give it on a matching basis. I will match every increased dollar coming from our trustees up to $25,000. But my gift has to be anonymous. I don't want people knowing it is me, and I do not want other organizations seeing my name as one of the large donors. You will report the challenge and monitor progress and tell board members how it is going. Let's make sure they know how much they will be leaving on the table if they do not ante up."

The board challenge was a great success. It not only increased board giving for the year, it also established a new level of giving that could be used for budgeting purposes in the years following. The trustees rose to the occasion, anonymity was preserved, and the executive director got the message across without being seen as its author.

Questions

1. Is the board fulfilling its giving requirements? Is there 100 percent participation? Is the giving level high enough?

2. Are there members of the board who for one reason or another are not required to give? Do the reasons for this nonparticipation appear to be valid ones, or should the policy be changed?

3. Are there explicit policies in place about giving? What are they? How and where are they expressed? How are they shared with existing and prospective board members?

4. Is there a minimum giving requirement? Is there a goal for the board as a whole? How do these change (and presumably rise) over time?

5. Are there board members who are willing to take on the problem of inadequate trustee giving? Are there ways the executive director can be helpful in the process, without jeopardizing important board relationships?

6. What more convincing arguments can be made to get board members to give? What incentives can be created to ensure that they give at the level at which they are capable?

8

CRACKING THE WHIP: GETTING TRUSTEES TO FUNDRAISE

Some executive directors struggle with trustees who do not make contributions, as we saw in the previous chapter. Others complain that their trustees do not give enough. But by far, the more universal challenge is trustees who do not fulfill their responsibility as fundraisers. Giving *and* getting is part of the mantra of trusteeship. Yet, when it comes to the getting part, many trustees simply refuse—or quietly avoid their obligations.

Doug was thrilled when he was invited to become executive director of one of the most prominent nonprofit organizations in his community. His board was made up of stellar names that were a mix of affluent individuals and corporate CEOs. Doug knew they were generous. The organization had just completed a successful capital campaign without ever going out to the public. The trustees themselves had provided all the money. They had built a new building, all with trustee money. "This seemed a slam dunk for me," Doug recalled years later. "In fact, it seemed too good to be true."

The reality hit soon after Doug assumed the reigns. While his board was indeed generous, they were busy people who believed their money obligations ended with their large contributions. And while this had been adequate for capital needs in conjunction with a new building, they were not adequate for the more mundane needs of operating and programming the building. The operating budget had increased substantially, but the annual contributions from Doug's trustees did not increase commensurately. Expanded fundraising was necessary, but when Doug mentioned this to the trustees, the response was: "That is why we hired you. We give. Your job is to get money from others. If you need help, hire somebody."

While Doug's situation was difficult, at least he had a board that was willing to contribute. Others, as we have seen, do not even do that. But just because his trustees were personally (or corporately) generous did not exempt them from their fundraising obligations. Quite simply, this is part of the trustee's role.

Once again, it is important to state that there are trustees who may be free from any requirement to raise money. The situations are not unlike those we have seen before: honorary or *ex officio* trustees who are exempted; those appointed by public officials according to statute who are not expected to raise money; or trustees for organizations that are not dependent on significant levels of contributions. These examples aside, though, fundraising is the special purview of a board.

Why should this fundamental obligation be so widely misunderstood or ignored? Some trustees simply are not well-informed. They believe they have been asked to serve for other reasons. Others subscribe to the common misperceptions that where an organization has professional fundraising staff (including, in some cases, an executive director skilled at raising money), the trustees do not have to be active in that area. Still others understand fundraising to be a board responsibility, but believe that as long as some trustees serve in that role, the problem is solved. Finally, there are those who know perfectly well what they are supposed to do, but simply choose not to.

So how does an executive director, faced with board members who will not participate in fundraising, overcome their resistance?

Some years ago, Jeanne, an experienced fundraiser and inspirational speaker, was invited to lead a conference seminar for executive directors on the topic of encouraging board members to fundraise. She was initially surprised by the invitation and cool to the subject matter. "This is not a good topic," she told the conference organizer. "Getting board members to fundraise is not the executive director's job. It is the job of the board president or other trustees. They have to light the fire and get their peers to be involved in the important work of fundraising."

The conference organizer disagreed, saying, "You know perfectly well that in many cases it will only happen if executive directors become involved. Help them figure out what specifically executive directors can and should do."

Eventually, Jeanne designed a seminar under the title of this chapter: "Cracking the Whip: Getting Board Members to Fundraise." To get good material in advance, Jeanne canvassed participants, asking a simple question: "What excuses do board members give for not fundraising?" The various responses were placed in a dozen categories that were dispiritingly familiar:

1. I don't know how to ask for money.
2. I don't feel comfortable asking for money.
3. Others are better at asking for money than I am.
4. I can't ask my friends for money.
5. I can't ask my family for money.
6. If I ask people for money, they will ask me.
7. I already gave.
8. I am too busy.

9. The executive director is a professional in this area.
10. The organization already has development staff.
11. I do other things for the organization.
12. I won't be successful.

Having seen the many manifestations of the problem, Jeanne was able to get participants to come up with common-sense solutions to how they could be addressed. Many of the executive directors were already using one or two of them, but collectively, they amounted to a veritable arsenal of strategies.

Let's start with the heart of the matter—the concern about asking for money. The first six of the twelve reasons for not fundraising all have the word "ask" in them. So clearly, many trustees simply do not understand the many aspects of the fundraising process, of which asking is just one part. They hear the term "fundraise," and it conjures up a picture of a bejeweled matron or a corporate titan sitting impatiently, drumming the arm of a chair, while the reluctant trustee begs for a handout. It is a frightening image for many trustees, especially those who have never thought about it before, so the first task is to dispel the image. The second is to replace it with a comprehensive picture of the fundraising process. That is an executive director's role.

As one executive director put it, "We have analyzed all the tasks that go into fundraising at our organization. Yes, making calls and asking someone for a gift is one job. But, there are so many others: working on our annual gala, or other fundraising events, is one large category. Personalizing direct mail letters and personally acknowledging gifts by writing thank you notes is another category (some of our younger trustees will send out emails). We also encourage our trustees to go through annual reports and programs of other local nonprofits and compile lists of their high-end donors and then secure addresses when possible so we can add them to our prospect list. Identifying acquaintances or family members who might be associated with corporations and foundations, working on a fundraising video, taking photographs at some of our programs that could be included in a brochure, helping to develop good ideas and copy for fundraising materials—the list goes on and on. Any of this can be counted toward discharging one's fundraising responsibilities."

"What we do is ask board members to rate these activities in order of preference. Once they do, we are well on our way toward developing an army of fundraising volunteers. We find that there are a lot of things that are part of fundraising that even our most recalcitrant volunteers are willing to do. And success in one area can often build confidence in another. You would be surprised how many of those who absolutely refused to ask for money are now comfortable doing so. It is my job as executive director (and that of my development director) to work with the group, finding their areas of interest and willingness and nurturing them."

Once trustees have chosen fundraising tasks, there is still the challenge of fulfillment. Many will sign up for things with the best will in the world and then discover they are too busy and put off the responsibility. Addressing this frustration can be as easy as developing written assignments with due dates and a master calendar that is shared with the entire board. Once again, it is the executive director who either performs this task, or in larger organizations with development staff, ensures that it gets done. Monitoring, reminding, and reporting is as important as developing the assignment sheets in the first place.

It remains the case that some board members will actually have to do some soliciting, and here the issue may be fear of the unknown and fear of failure. Looking at the list from Jeanne's workshop, many of the excuses board members gave centered around anxiety about the act of asking. Change that, and one is more likely to get volunteer askers.

A skilled executive director can begin the process of addressing the anxiety of asking by breaking it into finer-grain detail. What are people really worried about? As it turns out, in example after example, there are five important anxiety moments that trustees talk about:

- The first is the moment of setting up a fundraising appointment. What should they say and not say? How much should they acknowledge about it being a fundraising call? Would they get rejected before they even get an appointment?
- Second, there is the worry about how to start the conversation once they meet with a prospect. What should they talk about?
- Third is the moment of making the transition to the topic of fundraising. There can be great anxiety about doing that smoothly and without embarrassment.
- Fourth is the "ask" itself. Should they ask for a specific amount? Would the donor be insulted or angry if they did?
- Finally, there is the anxiety of knowing what to do when they get an answer, especially if that answer is no.

Helping trustees feel more confident about each of these anxious moments can go a long way toward making them willing to try. Practicing with them might well give them the confidence they need to get over the hump. Accompanying them on some initial calls will provide practice and even more confidence.

An executive director, especially one who is not particularly confident and experienced about these issues, may want to solicit help from a board member or an outside professional trainer. Or he or she may decide to pair less-experienced trustees with confident, experienced ones (or with a staff member). No board members should be forced to solicit friends or family if they do not want to, though all should be encouraged to serve as door openers for others. Since nothing succeeds like success, and the greatest inducement to persuading trustees to do more fundraising is to have them succeed the first few times, it is important to collect and disseminate success stories. Offering beginners low-hanging fruit to help them succeed on their initial forays can also serve as encouragement.

One of the most important misunderstandings is found in organizations that have professional development staff or even in those where the executive director is the only professional who raises money. Some inexperienced trustees, recognizing the expertise and competence of these individuals, may wonder what they can offer in fundraising. For starters, as we have seen, there are many tasks that do not require expertise. And there are others where the involvement of a board member is simply more appropriate. As volunteers, who are themselves giving time and money, their credibility may well be greater than salaried staff. In addition, their involvement in a task can serve as a compliment to a potential donor.

Again, it is the executive director who can help convey these messages, explaining what development staff members actually do and where they need help. Explaining the credibility that board members bring to the fundraising process puts the proposition of their involvement in the form of a compliment rather than a scold. It also builds a sense of teamwork that provides a strong and positive culture within the organization.

The case histories of Doug and Jeanne both have happy endings. Doug, the executive director with generous trustees who were unwilling to fundraise, was one of the individuals who had attended Jeanne's seminar, and he implemented many of the recommendations the group had come up with. Within a few years, every trustee in his organization was involved in some way in the fundraising effort, even if only peripherally, and each person's tasks were memorialized in development committee minutes. The chair of the development committee monitored and enforced the responsibilities as assigned. At the same time, the organization created a group called "the overseers," where those who did not wish to be involved in all of the responsibilities of governance, including fundraising, could go.

As for Jeanne, her "Cracking the Whip" conference seminar, the one she initially felt reluctant to present, was so popular that many other groups requested it, and she repeated it many times. Eventually, she built the topic into a fundraising course she taught at a local university. The topic of how an executive director can encourage board members to fundraise turned out to be an important one and served as another example of how an effective executive director can help individuals become more effective trustees.

Questions

1. Is there a general policy that trustees in the organization should be involved in fundraising? How is the requirement stated? If a policy does not exist, is the topic regularly discussed? Should an explicit written policy be developed?
2. If and when trustees refuse to get involved in fundraising, what reasons do they give? What are some strategies to address their concerns and fears?
3. Are fundraising assignments documented, scheduled, and put into a master calendar? Is there a system of monitoring, reminding, and addressing situations where work is not getting completed? Does the executive director get assistance from trustees in helping to deal with problem situations?
4. How are board members oriented to the comprehensive nature of fundraising and the many opportunities to do different tasks associated with it? Are there special orientation sessions for new trustees? Are there ways that individuals can opt for those areas where they will be most comfortable and successful?
5. Are there training opportunities for those who are willing to be solicitors? Are these sessions set up to address their anxieties? Are there experienced trustees or staff willing to

accompany inexperienced solicitors on calls, at least initially, until they have had some success?

6. Is the executive director sufficiently experienced and confident to carry out the functions involved in getting board members to become involved in fundraising? If not, are there ways that he or she can get more help?

9

UNDERSTANDING AND OVERSEEING THE FINANCES

In a nonprofit organization, who is supposed to be on top of the finances? Who needs to understand what is going on with current revenues and expenses, the budget, assets and liabilities, investments, and the financial operation itself? Does the board treasurer bear the most responsibility? Is it the executive director or another staff member? What about the finance committee, an investment committee of the board, or the executive committee? Or is it all of the trustees collectively?

In fact, everyone mentioned needs to be on top of the finances to a degree. But the level of understanding can vary, and the various individuals have different roles to play. Positive relationships between the executive director and the board will help to ensure that communication is effective, key information is properly shared, and decision making at various levels is well-synchronized.

On the board side:

- Legally, each and every trustee has a fiduciary oversight responsibility. Indeed, every trustee must be sufficiently cognizant of the financial condition of the organization so as to make prudent decisions. Each must know enough to cast reasonably informed votes on the budget, on financial activities, and on financial policy.

- The board treasurer, an officer of the corporation, is the designated board expert and must be especially vigilant about bringing before his or her fellow trustees any decision on which their insights, opinions, and votes are important. The treasurer is also responsible for ensuring that the actions of the staff in the financial area meet standards established by the board, appropriate tax filings are completed, and the annual audit takes place (if required). Working closely with the executive director and with an executive committee of the board on which the treasurer serves as an *ex officio* member, financial information can be evaluated and sifted such that only the most important items need go to the full board.

- In most organizations, even relatively small ones, the treasurer is assisted in these tasks by a group of trustees serving on a finance committee. These individuals generally have a special interest and expertise in the financial area and are willing to take the time to go into depth about financial issues.

- Separately, in cases where there are investments (such as an endowment), there is another group—an investment committee—most or all of whom are also trustees. On occasion, these individuals actually make decisions on the disposition of individual investments held by the corporation. More commonly, they oversee and monitor the work of one or more investment professionals and report back to the board, making recommendations for changes when they feel it is appropriate.

On the staff side:

- Financial staff must carry out the day-to-day financial operations, including transactions, accounting, and reporting. Financial staff generally interface with other staff members to ensure that they budget within parameters established by the board, stay within prescribed spending limits, and adhere to other financial policies and controls established by the board.

- As in other areas, the executive director serves as a key link between staff and board on financial matters. Ultimately, he or she is responsible for the staff's performance in connection with financial management and reporting. The executive director may also be the most informed leader with respect to long-range strategic financial planning, and the individual who is in the best position to answer questions and concerns from board members about the finances overall.

- In large nonprofits, where the financials are complex, there is often a senior director or vice president for finance immediately below the executive director on the organization chart to whom the executive director may delegate in the financial area, while still retaining ultimate responsibility.

With so many people concerned with finances, there will inevitably be areas of tension, although when there is trust and confidence on all sides, problems can generally be avoided. This is especially true in the relationship between the executive director and the treasurer, which is one reason why the selection of the right treasurer by the board is so critically important. This individual must be well-versed in financial matters and someone who can work well with others. The treasurer position should never be regarded as primarily honorific.

Sandra was an executive director who had particularly bad luck with treasurers in the various nonprofits she had led. At the first, the treasurer was an elderly man who had been passed over for the position of board president. The treasurer position was his consolation prize—always a bad sign. Unfortunately, he knew very little about finances in nonprofit organizations, and it fell to Sandra and her finance director to coach the individual, greatly adding to the time they would normally have spent. For each board meeting, they had to write out an oral presentation and indicate where votes needed to be taken, especially on policy issues. The board president, realizing that the treasurer was still angry at having been passed over for his position, was reluctant to intervene.

At her second organization, Sandra had the exact opposite problem. The treasurer, an accountant by profession, was a stickler for detail, asking for multiple presentations of financial statements, looking for back-up information, calling often with questions of dubious importance, and spending much time second-guessing the outside examiner conducting the annual audit. Once again, this involved a great deal of time, as well as Sandra's repeated interventions to defend the actions of her finance director, who was regularly criticized. The president tried to intervene, but the treasurer told him that he was only performing his fiduciary responsibilities as required by law, and unless the board removed him, he would go on doing what he had been doing. The president washed his hands of the whole problem.

Sandra's third experience was in some ways the most awkward. Her president and treasurer were at loggerheads. The president had served in the treasurer role before being elected president, and he continued to want the same level of involvement with the finances as he had previously had. He strenuously objected to changes the treasurer was requesting in financial reporting, and both appealed to Sandra to back their opinions.

In the end, Sandra came to realize that when considering an executive director position with a nonprofit, it was critical to interview both the president and the treasurer to gain an understanding of the personalities of the individuals. It was important to sense how they would work together, what their expectations would be of staff in the financial area, and what level of expertise and understanding they brought to their tasks. By the time Sandra moved once again, she was prepared, and her interviews proved fruitful. She wished that she had not spent the first twelve years of her career as an executive director without this key knowledge.

Another common area of potential tension has to do with the format for the presentation of financial statements. Some people will want to see numbers in mind-numbing detail. Others will want to see a few summary lines of revenue and expense so they can get a good overall understanding of what is going on. But even preparing something simple can be a challenge. In recent years, financial reports in nonprofit corporations have become confusing, partly because the requirements of the Financial Accounting Standards Board (FASB) often seem counterintuitive to a layman. As but one example, if an organization receives a multiyear grant or pledged contribution that is to be paid out over several years, the entire sum must be booked in the financial records as having been received in the first year, thus greatly inflating the actual cash taken in during that year. There are many other examples like this that so confuse some trustees (and some staff) that many will insist on an alternative version of the financial statements, at least for study and illustrative purposes.

But requests in this area often seem contradictory, and it is imperative for the executive director and treasurer to form a team to come up with a workable solution. "Give us more detail in the financial statements, we simply do not know what is going on," a trustee may exclaim one month. The next month, another trustee's complaint might be: "This stuff is way too complicated. I can't make head nor tail of it. Can't you simplify it, so we can figure out what is really going on?" Often, no single financial statement will please everybody, so multiple versions may be the only solution. The first one would be labeled "complete" and would follow all the accounting rules and would be the organization's "official" statement. It is the one that would go to the finance committee and be signed off on by the treasurer. It would be available to all board members if they wish to see it, but noncommittee members may rarely want to. Then there would be another version that goes to the trustees prior to each board meeting. It would include a cover sheet that explains the important trends in general, nontechnical terms, followed by a simple, one-page status report of revenues and expenses restated in layman's terms. It would be adjusted for anomalies like pledge payments and would give everyone a good sense of where things stood in general terms. There would always be copies of the more detailed official report available if a trustee says, "Where is the detail?"

Frustration levels can run high, and some of the concerns are often valid. Financial statements that come late are more than a frustration. They prevent trustees from doing their job of financial oversight in a timely way. Monthly statements should come within the month following (or on occasion, the month after that), except in the case of year-end statements that are more complicated and may require another few weeks. And when there are errors in the statements, it is enough to make the trustees rightfully apoplectic. One of the jobs of an executive director is to make sure the financial statements are accurate and on time.

Generally, in the case of nonfinancial areas, when trustee complaints seem excessive, it is up to the board president to make them "behave." But when it comes to financial statements, every trustee has a right—no, a duty—to understand what is going on and to insist on a report that clarifies the point. This is because of each trustee's fiduciary responsibility to ensure that the financial future of the organization is secure. No matter how many financial statements it takes, everyone should understand the financial position of the organization and make informed decisions about its budget and its financial affairs. Otherwise, the organization is looking for trouble.

Jane was a woman with considerable financial savvy who was very supportive of a nonprofit organization to which her young daughter had become attached. One day, she received a call.

The program in which her daughter was participating was not going to be renewed. In fact, the whole organization was going to go into hiatus. There were some serious financial problems that had to be sorted out.

Jane called some of the other parents. The cessation of activities was big news, but no one seemed to understand what had happened. There were no financial irregularities as far as they could tell—no one had absconded with any money. But there had also been no warning. Jane wanted to get to the bottom of what was happening. She wasn't so much angry as sad. Her daughter loved the program and had been planning to spend the summer in one of the organization's recreational facilities. Jane wondered if the program could be resurrected.

She called the executive director and the president of the board and asked whether she could help. Both were still uncertain about why they had run out of money. Jane offered to do some pro bono consulting. "Look, I do this kind of thing for a living with much larger organizations. This can't be rocket science. I am happy to help."

She began her work by asking questions of a lot of people. Most said that the problem was that the program was not drawing enough students. But as Jane investigated, she realized that was only the tip of the iceberg. The organization had an accumulated deficit of over a half million dollars. It had invested over $300,000 in capital items that it could not afford, increasing its liability 500 percent in just five years. It had been running an operating deficit, but because of a misunderstanding of the financial statements, people didn't realize it. The organization had no contingency line in the budget and had run out of cash reserves. Things, to put it mildly, were a mess.

But how had it happened? As the story was pieced together, the executive director had just been hired, and he assumed the board was on top of the finances. The board assumed he was. No one was steering the ship. And no one had sufficient financial expertise. Jane described it as having all the symptoms of the magic partnership between the executive director and board gone wrong. No one on the board was financially savvy enough to understand the financial situation. After all, there was always cash to pay the bills and purchase the capital items, at least until it ran out. The executive director had come to the organization at a time when there was money in the bank. Though he had a background in business and could have figured things out, he felt there were other pressing concerns to attend to. It was a fatal mistake.

After finally diagnosing all the problems, Jane, the board, and the executive director together discussed what was to be done. The problems would require both short-term and longer-term solutions. The organization had to come up with a conservative budget, it needed to pay off debt, and it needed to raise a cash reserve. A fundraising campaign was an obvious solution; people did love the organization after all. Jane's financial report, together with a financial rescue plan, gave donors assurances that their money would be safe, as long as new trustees with financial knowledge were appointed.

"On the theory that no good deed goes unpunished," said Jane, "I got appointed to the board and soon became treasurer." The executive director, at Jane's insistence, got some financial education. The organization established a finance committee, and for the next three years, Jane presided over monthly conference calls to do the reviews of the financials and make adjustments if the organization was falling short. It was all pretty basic stuff, but now the team was in place to carry it out.

And what about the executive director? He was completely chastened. He felt he had received a new lease on life and changed his behavior. He was pleased to have received the technical education and assistance, and thrilled that the board was giving more careful oversight and holding his feet to the fire. The first crisis had mainly happened on someone else's watch, though he didn't read the warning signs. Now he knew that this was his show. The magic partnership was restored.

Questions

1. How well-informed are the trustees about finances in the organization? Do they have sufficient information to make good decisions and carry out their fiduciary responsibilities? If not, what improvements can be made?

2. Is the board satisfied with the financial reports they receive? Do these reports include both sufficient detail and appropriate summary information that everyone can understand?

3. How active are the treasurer and the finance committee? Are they able to digest detailed information and make informed recommendations? Is there appropriate information sharing with the executive committee, such that its members can decide what needs to be forwarded to the full board for review and votes?

4. How well do the treasurer, the board chair, the finance director (if there is one), and the executive director work together? In what areas can the relationships be improved?

5. Does the executive director have a proper understanding of the finances and the financial management activities of the staff? Does he or she serve as a proper conduit between the financial activities of staff and board?

6. If the executive director's financial responsibilities are delegated to another staff person, is there sufficient communication, so that the staff leader is well-informed and able to respond to questions and concerns of the board?

10

PLANNING FOR THE FUTURE

A planning process is an opportunity for many people connected with a nonprofit organization to think expansively about its future. These include those involved in governance and management, constituents, volunteers, staff, funders, community and field leaders, all of whom may have opinions and ideas. Though it can be a challenge to consider and accommodate all of their divergent viewpoints, an open and inclusive process is generally desirable. It leads to a sense of broad ownership of a strategic plan, and often, people who will be willing to help pay for it. But it can be cumbersome, and at times, broad inclusiveness can derail a process and seriously delay a result.

Two individuals are key players in ensuring that the planning process is a success—the board president and the executive director. Executive directors are like orchestra conductors who know their players' capabilities and talents and can gauge the best way to come up with a harmonious product. They also start with another great advantage. They have detailed information and knowledge about most aspects of the organization or know how to get it. But executive directors also start with a disadvantage. Unlike orchestra conductors who are unabashedly in charge of the players, executive directors are not, especially when it comes to planning. Planning is the special province of the board, and the trustees hold the legal power to approve or disapprove a plan. That is why the board president is so important. He or she must corral the trustees and shepherd them to ultimate consensus.

The board president oversees a group of individuals—the trustees—who, in their oversight role, must be heavily involved in planning. While they do not have the detailed knowledge that the executive director and staff do, they have a broader view of community concerns and are less encumbered by the actual or perceived self-interest of a salaried workforce. The board's role includes setting policy and direction, articulating mission and vision statements and the organization's values, and laying out its general goals. The staff may be better positioned to design the particulars of action steps, timelines, and budgets. But even here, the trustees must consider recommendations, discuss them, decide whether they are prudent, and "bless" the plan with a formal vote of approval.

So, a good planning process has more than one leader. The board president should ensure that there is trustee consensus around broad directions, and the executive director will tend to the finer-grain detail. In the real world, it is not such a clean division. It is the rare executive director who is content to leave mission statements, goals, and general directions up to the board. Doing so can constrain organizational aspirations on the one hand (there will always be conservative trustees who do not like change), or lead to wild-goose chases on the other (where some trustees make unrealistic appraisals of what the organization can and should do). On the other hand, executive directors should never make assumptions about what the board wants, even at the detail level. Their tricky assignment is to ensure that in instilling their and the staff's own point of view, they do not appear to be controlling the process. The board, in turn, must make sure that the staff is being realistic in its design for the future.

Liesl was executive director of a successful nonprofit, and her organization had recently received a windfall grant that would allow for a major expansion of facilities, programs, and services. Assuming that her board was content with the mission statement, she and her senior staff set out to develop a blueprint for the future. The result was an imaginative plan for how they would expend the new funds and grow the organization. She sent the resulting document to a hastily appointed planning committee in a multicolored, printed presentation. Liesl's expectation was that the document was sufficiently strong that the committee would endorse it for approval at the next board meeting.

At the committee meeting, Liesl took members through a PowerPoint presentation and began laying out the plan details. She had not gotten beyond the fourth slide before many questions and concerns were raised. Had the staff really thought through the issues? Were the facility plans realistic for the long term? Were all the potential partnerships carefully explored? The planning committee was clearly not happy, and Liesl did not complete the presentation. It was obvious the committee was not going to endorse what they were reviewing, and without their approval, there was no point in taking it to the full board.

Was it substance or process? Did Liesl and her staff really get things wrong, or did they leave out some crucial consultative steps? Probably, it was a little of both. First, Liesl had taken for granted that the big picture items were in place—mission, vision, values. Then she had assumed it was the staff who had the expertise to develop the details of the planning document, which would be fairly technical, so there was no point in involving board members. Her thinking was that the trustees' role would be merely to suggest refinements and then approve the plan. But the trustees had a different view. They wanted to be more than a rubber stamp.

Several years later, as Liesl's organization was taking on a major planning process once again, her approach was completely different. She now realized how critical board involvement would be if her vision, and that of the staff, was to be accepted and endorsed. She utilized various trustees with appropriate interest and experience at key moments as she and staff developed details of the plan. Particularly successful was her decision to ask some trustees to present portions of the staff's work to the full board, giving it a level of credibility that had previously been lacking. The board, in turn, in a far more trusting mood, invited staff into conversations about mission, vision, and values. As Liesl herself later admitted, "At first, my willingness to change my approach was all about strategy—I wanted the board to go along with our work. But in the end, I realized that the greater integration of board and staff in planning actually made the product better."

How do executive directors avoid the pitfalls of the perception that they are railroading the planning process? How can they ensure that their views are strongly represented without the appearance of unwarranted control? An effective board president can be invaluable. This individual's role is two-fold: to ensure that the trustees are very much involved, and to make sure that they do not derail or hold up the process.

One mechanism that is effective is to utilize a planning committee of the board. Often this is made up exclusively of trustees, but occasionally other community members or volunteers who can provide important insights are invited. The executive director generally participates, and from time to time, staff members may be brought in for special purposes or information. The board president should not chair the planning committee. His or her role is to keep things moving, so a perception of objectivity and distance from the process allows the president to appear independent and more able to work to get competing camps to compromise. In many cases, the president does not even serve on the committee, but stays in touch and on top of things through the head of the planning committee (another trustee) and the executive director. Most board presidents will have opinions about the plan—often strong ones—but they can express these behind the scenes.

For some organizations, another way to ensure all parties feel their opinions are being heard is to hire an outside consultant. This individual can help design and coordinate a deliberative process involving planning committee members, other trustees, staff, funders, field experts, and constituents. Having a consultant who is able to distill ideas, summarize field trends, and frame planning issues can deflect criticism from the other key players—board president, executive director, and head of the planning committee—as well. It allows executive directors to manage many of the details of the process and instill key ideas without appearing to control it. A planning committee can thrash out ideas in an open and deliberative way. The full board can weigh in from time to time. The process can have the integrity of being open to information from many sources. The consultant will often meet with the executive director, board president, and the head of the planning committee to ensure that each is dealing effectively with its constituency, keeping them informed and keeping the planning process moving in sync.

It is a mistake to think that in strategic planning, everyone needs to have a hand in everything. That is when things get messy and plans get delayed or shelved. Everyone should get a shot at some point in expressing his or her views, but the process must be designed so that a few people cannot gum up the works just because they feel strongly about one thing or another and won't let go. Indeed, as strategic plans move toward their final adoption and recommendations get firmed up, the opportunities increase for the process to get derailed. The board knows it holds the power to approve or disapprove a plan, and the minority opinions of some trustees may harden. One or a few may see chances slipping away to get what they want, or old hostilities may flare up. A single trustee or a small group can waste a great deal of time grandstanding and holding up the process. This is the moment when board presidents must exercise their leadership, either by quiet persuasion, or if that doesn't work, a more mechanistic solution for freeing up time for other discussions and for garnering approval.

George was the president of the board of a local nonprofit organization that was moving toward the completion of a planning process. He was troubled by the fact that three of his trustees were taking up much time focusing on pet peeves and issues in discussions of the plan. Others were getting irritated. George felt he needed to get past these long digressions without offending the individuals, two of whom were major donors.

As it happened, George was to testify at a city council meeting the week before a critical board meeting to discuss that plan. He was supposed to give some expert testimony on a building project he favored that had no bearing on the nonprofit. He examined the city council agenda and saw that his item was quite far down the list. He settled in for a long meeting, letting his mind wander to his board problem. Yet within ten minutes, he was shocked to hear his name called. He fumbled around, grabbed his papers, and hurried up to the lectern. He had been completely unprepared for the rapid call-up.

When the meeting ended, George turned to the assistant city manager and asked him why things had moved so quickly. "Well, they approved the consent calendar and you were next." George had never heard of a consent calendar. What he learned was that on city council agendas, the items that most city councillors agreed upon would be put on a list called a consent calendar, and all the items would be voted through without debate at the beginning of the meeting, unless there were a vote to remove one or more items for discussion.

Voila, George's perfect solution for the planning process! Here was a way to keep most trustees satisfied most of the time by avoiding endless talk about what the great majority of people had already agreed to. George met with the executive director and planning committee chair. They divided the plan into sections by subject area and action steps and sent the draft to board members. Each was asked to indicate in advance those items they agreed with, those they disagreed with, or those they wished to discuss. Except in cases where 20 percent or more of the trustees identified items that they either disagreed with or wished to discuss, everything would be put on a consent calendar and voted on at the outset of the meeting without discussion. The result was amazing. Instead of the long meeting with dreaded discussion about someone's pet peeve or wish, the board discussed only four substantive items, resolved them, and approved the plan in record time

Questions

1. How inclusive should a planning process be for the organization? Besides trustees and staff, are there others whose opinions matter—funders, volunteers, constituents, community and field leaders? How will they be involved?

2. How involved will the board be in the process? What role will the board president play? Is there a planning committee that will solicit and represent the views of the trustees?

3. How will the staff be involved? How can the executive director ensure that the detailed knowledge and experience of the staff enriches and informs the process?

4. Will a consultant be used? If so, how can this individual help bring about consensus and move the process along on schedule?

5. What is the timeline for final approval? What steps will lead to a final vote? Will it be necessary or desirable to utilize a consent calendar approach?

11

NO SURPRISES, PLEASE

If there is one thing some executive directors have a problem learning, it is that board members do not like surprises—even good ones. Problems can emerge when an executive director inadvertently fails to pass on essential information to a board or does not request permission to take an action that trustees feel requires consultation.

But truth be told, there are times when executive directors know they should consult with the board and simply decide not to do so. The reasons can come from the best of impulses. They are impatient to get things done and know that the trustees may dither. A funding opportunity may have a deadline that should not be missed. In some cases, they figure they will risk going ahead, take some action, and deal with the consequences later. They can often get away with this approach a few times. But the behavior is generally not appreciated and can come back to haunt them, leading to a tighter leash than they started with.

Andy had been in his job as executive director for four years, leading a regional service and funding organization. His nonprofit organization was supported by six state agencies with additional funding supplied by the federal government. Representatives of the state agencies served on his board. Andy had discussed with them the idea of bringing in additional funding from regional corporations for the organization's programs. It made perfect sense, since his organization could play a role in helping corporations distribute their grant funds to organizations big and small, saving their staffs from having to do quality assessments and administration (Andy jokingly called it "one stop shopping"). Some peer organizations were doing this elsewhere around the country. Andy felt that his organization should follow their lead.

When he raised the idea in a board meeting, the reaction was tepid. Since the largest funders were state agencies, there was some concern that the impact of the public money would be diluted with private funds. Then there was the question of fundraising competition: would money be taken out of the general pool that was supporting Andy's constituents and given to Andy to distribute, essentially robbing Peter to pay Paul? The questions went on and on. Andy caught the eye of one of his most enlightened board members who was basically in support of the idea. He shrugged his shoulders and shook his head. It looked like Andy was in for a long fight.

But Andy wasn't in the mood for waiting. He decided to make a few exploratory inquiries and hired a fundraising consultant out of his discretionary budget to help identify some prospects and make some calls. Despite the fact that he had proposed the idea (or maybe because of it), he was not prepared for the enthusiasm he encountered. A lot of corporate giving officers were impressed with the reach of Andy's organization and its ability to find and fund small, high-quality organizations. In one case, the corporate giving officer for one of the region's largest utilities offered him an initial grant on the spot. "Here's what I want," he said. "We will give you an initial grant of $30,000 to test the concept. I want you to redistribute it for us. The only stipulation is that we get joint credit for the gift and that one of our local reps is present to deliver the check. We will arrange a photographer to be at each check-giving event."

Andy reminded his new corporate friend that this initial meeting had only been exploratory in nature, to test out a new idea, and he would have to present the offer to his board. But he couldn't imagine how the trustees could object. Then, instead of waiting for the next board meeting, he impatiently sent a letter to the individual trustees, telling them of their good fortune, and asking for a vote of approval by phone or email.

The reaction was instantaneous, and it was not pretty. The trustees were furious. Andy had boxed them into a corner. They could either say yes, which many of them did not want to do, or they could say no and look stupid and ungrateful to one of the region's most generous funders. In the end, they said yes and gave Andy a dressing down and a warning. But once he had let the genie out of the bottle, other corporate funders heard about the arrangement and wanted to climb aboard. Andy had prevailed. It had been dicey, but he had gotten what he wanted.

Unfortunately though, the whole experience left a bad taste in the mouths of the trustees. Their trust in Andy had been shaken. They shortened his leash. They insisted on more regular reporting and consultation. They gave him a further warning. He had won the battle and lost the war. Indeed, it was the first step in a growing deterioration of the partnership that led to Andy's departure two years later.

In a healthy relationship between boards and executive directors, each side generally shares their ideas, impressions, and concerns with the other. When communication falters, the executive director may not necessarily be the one at fault. It is true that the executive director may not always be totally open. But situations where boards keep things from their executive directors can be equally damaging to an effective partnership. In these cases, the problem is a bit more complex. There are things that the board must keep in confidence. Boards collectively serve as employers and supervisors of executive directors, and because there are many trustees on a board, their conversations about an executive director's performance need to be carried on in private, and ongoing confidentiality needs to be respected. Eventually, feedback should be shared, but individual comments of trustees should not be for attribution, and a response should represent collectively the opinions of the group.

It is when other topics are not shared with the executive director that a trusting relationship can be undermined. The sense of secrecy can be demoralizing, and it can chip away at an executive director's confidence. Sometimes this apparent secrecy is unintended, or the reason for it is necessary, but does not involve the executive director's performance.

Ginny was an executive director whose confidence was shaken when the board started going into executive session at the end of each board meeting. Then, she learned of a secret board meeting that was being held on a Saturday, when a trustee inadvertently said he looked forward to seeing her there. Once Ginny learned of this, she started to wonder what was being discussed behind her back. She thought she observed discussions that would happen out of earshot or that would cease when she entered a room. Topics would come up at the board meeting and there would be awkward silences. She was feeling odd about it, then angry, then scared. She wondered what they were saying and whether it was about her performance. She began to judge which trustees were her allies and which were her enemies. She wondered if she should be proactive and round up her troops.

Since no minutes were kept of the executive sessions or the secret board meetings (she assumed there were more than one), Ginny grew increasingly restive and worried. She began exploring options for other jobs. She discussed the situation with friends. She double-checked her employment agreement and the organization's personnel policies. In other words, she spent a lot of energy and time on an activity tangential to the core business of the organization.

Finally, she could take it no longer. She went to her president. "Look," she said, "I don't know what is going on. But whatever it is, I don't think it is healthy. If I am not performing to your expectations, I want that feedback. We need to have a more open relationship if it is going to be a healthy one."

Ginny was totally unprepared for his reaction. He burst out laughing. In the end, the issues being discussed had nothing to do with Ginny or her performance. There was a potential pending legal matter that could have a significant impact on the corporation, and the board had wanted to shield Ginny from any involvement in case litigation was involved. Ginny had lost lots of sleep in the interim over a bogus concern.

"Okay," said the president once the air had been cleared. "From here on out, we have a deal. You will not keep secrets from us, and we will not keep secrets from you. At the very least, I should have told you what was going on and why, so you could have been spared the worry."

When executive directors need to be informed, communication procedures tend to be fairly clear. Once the message is delivered to him or her, the deed is done. But when the communication needs to go the other way, things are sometimes less clear. For example, while the board president will in many cases be the conduit for things the executive director needs to convey to the board as a whole or for requests that need to be cleared, in some cases, it may be more appropriate to talk with the treasurer on matters of financial import or someone else in the organization, such as a committee chair. In each case, the board member is responsible for determining whether other trustees need to know and how the information will be further distributed.

The best opportunity for each side to share their concerns about apparent secrecy is during the board's annual personnel evaluation of the executive director. Trustees can use a simple instrument to rate the executive director in each area of his or her job description according to a ten-point scale and then provide comments below each rating. One of these should certainly be "communication with the board." The president can then average the scores, summarize the comments, send the document to the executive director, and the two can meet to discuss it. At such a meeting, executive directors can address the findings and offer some observations of their own about board performance in general and any concerns about communication specifically.

Interestingly, boards tend to place great weight on the issue of communication. An executive director may receive high marks for leadership, fundraising, and staff supervision, but if the area "works well and communicates effectively with board" is found wanting, this can signal that something is fundamentally broken. Consultation is not some nicety that executive directors and boards need to follow. It is not a question of good manners. It is the essence of an effective working partnership.

Questions

1. Does the executive director routinely pass on important information to the board? Does he or she seek permission for pursuing new areas of activity that are part of the board's purview?

2. What are the mechanisms for communicating with the board to ensure that information will be assessed and passed on to the trustees as necessary? Aside from the board president, are there others with whom the executive director should communicate in specific situations?

3. Has the board done everything possible to respond quickly to executive director requests when important opportunities or concerns have to be addressed?

4. How can the annual performance review be used as a way to ensure that there is good communication between the executive director and the board?

5. What are the topics and situations in which boards need to preserve confidentiality of communication? Are there ways that they can diffuse anxiety on the part of the executive director by being open about these areas?

6. When personnel issues are being discussed, is the board open about how the process will work and how and when the executive director will be informed of the results?

12

COMING AND GOING

Some executive directors stay too long—others not long enough. In both cases, the board is often to blame.

Consider the executive directors who depart before anyone wants them to. Sometimes they leave to take a better job. Sometimes they burn out. Sometimes it is a question of personalities clashing. In many of these cases, the departure could have been delayed or prevented.

Trustees can offer all kinds of incentives to a high-quality executive director to encourage him or her to stay. Among them are:

- A higher salary
- More generous benefits
- Release time for professional opportunities
- A sabbatical
- More administrative assistance
- A retention bonus
- A deferred compensation package that rewards them for staying.

Michael ran a nonprofit organization in North Carolina. The organization had been in serious trouble before he arrived, and his job initially was to turn it around, reestablish credibility with local corporate leadership, and rebuild relationships with constituents. Michael did all of this and more. In partnership with his board, he undertook a comprehensive planning process involving the wider community that resulted in many well-funded new programs. He presided over the building of new facilities. He attracted public and private investment from outside the region. He was put on the board of the local community foundation. His board knew that they had a winner.

But the trustees worried. How could they keep Michael? Many larger communities had a history of poaching and trying to lure away good talent with offers of more money. Some of the jobs were quite prestigious. Michael's board wanted to do everything possible to make sure he stayed. They knew his wife had a good job at a local college and that his three kids were thriving in the local schools. But they feared that wasn't enough to hold an ambitious young man. The personnel committee put together an emergency plan that was approved by the board in executive session. The president then talked to Michael.

First, the board decided to increase Michael's salary and benefits immediately and dramatically. True, it wasn't the end of the contract period, but the board agreed he was well worth the investment in terms of the grants he was bringing in alone. The increase in salary was accompanied by a special benefit Michael had always wanted—a company car. The new package sent a message that was unmistakable. They thought Michael was doing a great job and should be rewarded.

Second, the trustees encouraged Michael to accept any appointments he wished to with national service organizations and on national panels and to consider the time he spent on these projects as part of his work time for his nonprofit. Sure, he would be away a lot, but this prestige could only enhance his standing with his peers and enhance his own feeling of self-worth. It would also, at the same time, enhance the organization's standing, and Michael's new contacts would increase opportunities for national funding for the organization back home.

Third, the board told Michael to hire an experienced personal assistant in addition to the clerical person he already had, someone who could help him manage his many work commitments, his schedule, and could speak with authority to high-level individuals, like board members and corporate CEOs.

Finally, they told him that at the end of the fiscal year, they wanted him to consider taking a sabbatical to recharge his batteries. It would be four years that he had been with the organization, and as far as the board was concerned, the five-month paid leave would be entirely justified. The only condition was that Michael would agree to work for the organization for at least eighteen more months when he returned.

Michael was surprised and grateful. He had not asked for any of this. He had been considering asking for an increase in salary, but nowhere near what was being offered. When recruiters called, he said he was happy and not interested in considering another job at this time.

Meanwhile, another strategy was in the works. The compensation committee of the board put together a special offer that provided yet another incentive for Michael to stay. At the end of his sabbatical, they set up a deferred compensation plan. It worked in the following way. Each year over the ensuing five years, the board would put an amount equal to 15 percent of Michael's salary into a fund. At the end of five years, if Michael were still working for the organization, the money was his. If he left the organization at any time during the five years, the funds would revert to the organization and be put into its endowment fund.

Not every talented executive director's board is in a position to do all the things Michael's organization did for him. But some seem completely oblivious of the talent they have in their executive director and are surprised when the individual, who they have been taking for granted, departs. It is a particular problem for long-time executive directors who simply are given routine raises each year. Because they have often started from a low base, these increases do not reflect the merit of their performance. So, it is easy for another organization to make a better offer. Some trustees will think, "Well, this person has been here a long time; she won't want to leave." But they will often be surprised.

The same problem often occurs with executive directors who have been promoted from within. Unlike outsiders, these individuals may have little bargaining power when first offered the job. Occasionally, they are given the top job only after more desirable outside candidates have turned it down, or the board determines that hiring outsiders will be too expensive. The result may well be an underestimation of the individuals' merits, especially if they grow in the job. Trustees need to pay attention and ask whether the original assessment—and the compensation level for it—is fair and continues to be enticing.

Martha was an executive director who had originally joined her organization as a volunteer. She was a stay-at-home mother, but believed in the organization's mission and its programs. The trustees rewarded her volunteer efforts by appointing her to a seat on the board, where she came into her own and excelled. As her children grew older, she made a decision to return to work, and this coincided with an opening on the staff of the organization—a director of education position. Martha applied and was offered the job. In this role, she met with and worked with several key donors and brought in one of the largest gifts ever recorded for the organization. When the development director left, Martha was promoted to his position, and it was only a matter of time before she applied for and became the executive director.

So far, Martha felt thrilled by her good luck. So did the board. After all, she could do the job, and they could pay her 20 percent less than the previous executive director based on her lack of experience and skills. They told Martha they had every intention of raising her salary commensurate with her growing experience. But each year at budget time, there just wasn't enough money in the budget to do anything except give Martha a cost-of-living increase. And when her replacement as development director eventually left, the board wondered whether she might do both jobs until the budget situation improved. Martha reluctantly agreed.

As the situation continued to deteriorate, no one on the board worried too much. After all, Martha had been lucky to land such a good job in what was a small community without a lot of comparable opportunities, and they believed she wasn't going anywhere. Her kids were still going to the local school, and her husband worked locally and was unlikely to want to relocate. At some point, the board was going to make things right with her. For now, the trustees agreed, there was nothing that could be done.

But unbeknownst to the board, a competing nonprofit was courting Martha. The group did it informally at first—some discreet inquiries were made by a board member. Then some clandestine meetings were held, and the trustees of the new organization told Martha that she should name her price. She laughed it off, but she was torn. Her son was preparing to go to an expensive college, and she had two more children in high school and on their way to college. On a lark, she decided to name what was for her an extravagant price. In fact, the salary she quoted only seemed extravagant to her. Her board had been so stingy for so long, and she had become so significantly underpaid, that the new organization was willing to meet her price, and they threw in an attractive retirement package. Martha agreed to make the move.

When Martha announced her decision to her board, they were shocked. Many were still of the mind that they had done Martha a favor by hiring her, and she was being ungrateful. Others asked why she had not told them about the offer so they could match it. At that point, Martha knew she had made the right decision. If the only way she could command their attention and appreciation was to get a competing offer from someone else, they didn't deserve her.

⌄

It should be said that many boards assume, incorrectly, that rewarding an executive director will be costly, and if the organization does not have the funds, it is simply out of luck. It is true that many of the proposed actions in this chapter involve money. But sometimes all it takes is sincere and public appreciation. Special thank-you events can be planned, especially on an important anniversary with the organization. The executive director can be invited to board members' homes for social events, especially if these provide an opportunity to mix with and meet community leadership or a particularly distinguished guest. Even official statements of appreciation recorded in the board minutes can make someone feel special. There is no upside to treating treasured executive directors as mere employees, simply doing their jobs. Even if they stay, their resentment at such treatment can ultimately undermine the potential good they can do for the organization.

Finally, no matter how effective a board will be in retaining good executive directors or in having ample time to plan for their replacements, when the time comes for them to go, there will be occasions when executive directors will depart with little notice (Martha's situation was just such a case). Steps must be taken immediately to fill the gap while a replacement is sought. Commonly, an interim executive director will be chosen from the staff, or a board member may step in.

These situations have their own inherent dangers, aside from the obvious one—whether the individual can do the job effectively. In organizations that have thought about the issue and have a succession plan, the individual will have shared in enough of the key decisions and responsibilities of executive director to know what the job entails. Filling in for a time may feel natural and comfortable, especially if the board provides plenty of support (including making sure the individual, if a staff person, is not expected to do the equivalent of two jobs—the executive director's and his or her own).

Another challenge comes once the permanent executive director is hired, assuming the interim does not become the permanent. Having tasted the power and prestige that comes with the top staff position, becoming familiar with the issues, developing a new relationship with the board—all these things can make it difficult for the interim executive director to return to the old position. Especially dangerous is the tendency to second-guess and criticize the incoming executive director, who is, after all, just learning about the organization and the job. Being sensitive to the challenges of "letting go" should be something that is discussed at the time of the initial appointment and again when the permanent replacement is chosen. Board members should monitor the situation and attend to it in the early months of the new regime in order to facilitate a smooth transition.

Questions

1. How valuable is the executive director to the organization? How high a price in time, money, prestige, or community opinion would be paid if the executive director left?

2. Has any effort been made to determine what comparable positions pay both locally and nationally? If the current salary and benefits are well below par, has anything been done to start rectifying the problem? Has any thought been given to a deferred benefits package?

3. Has the board considered offering release time, either for national meetings or a sabbatical, to the executive director?

4. Does the executive director have proper help in the office? Does he or she spend too much time on mundane matters because of inadequate support?

5. If the executive director has had a long tenure or was promoted from within, is there a procedure for regularly assessing whether he or she is being treated fairly?

6. What other perks that do not cost money have been considered to reward the executive director? Are there ways that appreciation can be made obvious and made public?

13

NOT SOON ENOUGH

Sometimes, executive directors have to be let go for any number of reasons. Doing so is a key responsibility of the board. Firing an executive director is rarely a happy process, but it can be made easier if the grounds for doing so are clear, such as malfeasance or gross incompetence. In cases where laws are broken or the executive director's behavior countermands important officially documented policies (such as disclosing critical and sensitive confidential information), dismissal can be immediate. For incompetence, the process may be more drawn out. Three things are essential:

- There has to be a job description that lays out areas of responsibility and expectations of performance.
- There has to be a regularly scheduled evaluation that allows the board to provide feedback on job performance, raise concerns when appropriate, and lay out expectations for addressing those concerns.
- There has to be a documented series of steps that leads from a negative evaluation to dismissal if this proves necessary.

In many cases, encouraging executive directors to depart voluntarily is more desirable than firing them, especially if the firing will become public and acrimonious. Amicable separations protect both the individuals involved and the organizations. In an individual's case, the need to find another job and preserve a good reputation is often worth a great deal. In the organization's case, reputation is also important. A firing can lead outsiders (including funders) to lose faith in an organization. For both parties, there can be strong economic incentives to make the parting appear natural and positive at best, or at least not acrimonious.

Consider the case of Manny, whose repeated lapses of good judgment led to a decision on the part of the board to terminate his appointment as executive director. The situation involved inappropriate suggestions, first to one and then to a second female staff member, that they become involved with him in an extramarital relationship. Manny had been careful to keep the suggestions light and indirect, and despite the fact that the individuals complained to the board president, neither was willing to accuse Manny of harassment on record. Neither had any intention of taking any legal action unless the board refused to act, and even then they were reluctant, though both threatened to leave the organization. What they wanted was for the situation to stop. The first time there was a complaint, Manny was invited to meet privately with the board president, and the two agreed to consider what had happened a "misunderstanding." But the president issued a written warning on behalf of the board, and when the situation recurred a year later, and the accusations proved accurate, the board took more drastic action. They voted to terminate Manny's employment as executive director.

No one involved, not Manny, the accusers, or the board, wanted the situation to go public. The board, on the advice of an attorney, judged that legal harassment was not at issue, especially since neither accuser was willing to say it was. Manny and the board quickly agreed on an amicable separation with nondisclosures on both sides. Manny would resign and would depart immediately, utilizing unused paid vacation days so that he would still be paid for another three weeks. Benefits would also continue until his final day on the payroll.

Because the accusers were not interested or willing to bring legal charges against Manny or to go public in any way, because Manny had cooperated fully with the board, did not resist its decision, and resigned voluntarily, and because there had never been any other instance of inappropriate behavior or poor performance, the action of the board felt measured and appropriate. Certain members of the board felt the actions had been too harsh; others, too lenient. But in the end, all agreed that a quiet departure was in everyone's best interest.

For many reasons, it is often best to encourage an executive director to resign, unless there is clear legal malfeasance, in which case firing is an important public statement. In other situations, the board can offer incentives to allow the transition to be quieter and more positive. From the executive director's point of view, a financial severance package can be a very attractive incentive. Just as important to both parties is what each will say about the other after the parting. While the organization cannot promise to lie about the executive director's performance in the job, it can either agree to a nondisclosure agreement, in which neither side says anything about the other, or to talk only about those aspects of job performance that were positive. Enforcement of such agreements is not easy, though in a reciprocal agreement, both parties know that if one side breaches, the other is free to answer in kind.

A more challenging situation occurs when the reasons for a dismissal are less clear and are based on board consensus that it is simply time for a change. Long-time, successful executive directors can be a particular challenge. Firing them may not be a viable alternative, given long-time support and admiration for them; encouraging them to move on without public acrimony is the goal.

Remember the old adage about guests and fish? After a week, you probably don't want either of them around your house. When it comes to executive directors, they too can often overstay their welcome. And the longer they have been in the job, often the harder it is to get rid of them, even when it is clear to people close to the organization that it is time to go. Various things can make a forced or encouraged departure difficult: if executive directors are popular, if they were once superstar leaders, if they founded their organizations—in any of these cases, boards will sometimes throw up their hands, not wanting to appear to be the bad guys in a confrontation with a beloved figure. Sometimes, the personnel manual will make it especially difficult to dismiss an executive director, especially one who hasn't displayed gross failure in the job.

But since one of the key areas of responsibility for boards is ensuring that their organizations have the best executive directors possible, this means not only finding good ones and monitoring their performance, but getting them to leave. Pages and pages are written about how to fire the incompetents or those who are engaged in illegal activity, but this is relatively easy compared to moving someone along who has simply overstayed his or her welcome.

Jesse was an exemplary figure in his field, an executive director whose organization was three years shy of celebrating its fiftieth anniversary—all under his leadership. Jesse was widely respected. He had established important relationships with major donors. He was the subject of a film celebrating his exemplary work. He had chaired his national service organization and received its lifetime achievement award. Locally, he served on boards of other nonprofits, and he often spoke at Rotary and other organizations. He was a popular guy.

Behind the scenes, though, things were not so rosy. It was well-known that employees were increasingly complaining about Jesse, and some of that was leaking to the public. Many trustees were also unhappy. Age was creeping up on Jesse. He was not as sharp as he had once been. His hearing had deteriorated, but he refused to wear a hearing aid, which meant that he missed a lot in meetings, and that affected his work. Though he had email, he checked it only sporadically and would inadvertently delete things that were important. Phone calls went unanswered. Invoices sat on his desk for weeks, and the bookkeeper would get irate phone calls. Jesse had always said that invoices should be routed to him first, just as they had been in the organization's earliest days. When the bookkeeper pointed out that the budget had increased twenty-fold since then and Jesse was unmoved, she quietly asked people to send duplicates to her and mentioned this to the treasurer of the board.

Things came to a head when the board hired a consultant to conduct a feasibility study for a fiftieth anniversary capital campaign. Interviews with major donors consistently focused on Jesse and the future. What was the succession plan? How soon would Jesse be leaving, and what was the process for finding his replacement? More generally, what was the vision for the future? Was there a strategic plan document? Jesse had always maintained that the organization needed to be entrepreneurial, and he had resisted any kind of serious formal planning. But the donors were clear: they were not going to give to an endowment or make other serious investments in the organization's future when that future (including the next generation of leadership) was so unclear.

Jesse and his organization were fortunate in one respect. There were people on the board who were prepared to handle the situation with finesse, delicacy, and firmness. Many had seen trustees of other organizations flounder in analogous situations, and they wanted to solve this dilemma before it ripped apart the organization or divided the community.

The board president, an executive with a Fortune 100 company, recounted what happened: "It was an interesting situation. Jesse had recruited me to the board. I liked him and respected him, and I am quite sure it was vice versa. He had pushed hard for me to become president. Now our relationship would be tested.

"The way I laid out the situation to him was on the basis of legacy. He had created something quite marvelous, and we needed to make sure that, together, we saw it thrive well into the future. That was going to take money, and the feedback we were getting from donors was that they needed to see a plan and a clear road toward succession.

"I told him I was going to initiate a strategic planning process, and though he was welcome to be a part of it, it was going to be led by the board, and we would use an outside consultant. 'It is not that we don't have confidence in you, Jesse,' I said, 'but we, the board, need to own the vision going forward when you are no longer around. We want to preserve the best of what you have created *and* we need to look forward. Part of what we are asking the consultant to tell us is what does best-practice look like in this field, and what are others doing?'

"Initially, Jesse was upset. I told him that he and I needed to continue to talk privately, and if he wanted to yell at me, well, that was fine. But for the good of the organization, we should keep it between us. We went ahead and initiated the planning, and it did make him uncomfortable, especially because we approved some directions that he clearly disagreed with, but were reflective of new directions in the field.

"In time, we discussed his retirement plans. He said he would like to stay on indefinitely in some capacity, even if he stepped down as executive director. This was the diciest moment.

I asked him how he would feel were he a new executive director if the long-time legend was still around second-guessing his every move. 'We want to honor your achievements, Jesse; we want to raise money in your honor and name a major scholarship for you, and we want to provide a little extra for you for your years in retirement. You've earned it.' I then talked about a two-year time frame.

"Jesse reluctantly agreed. At first he complained to many of his friends that he was being forced out. Then he realized that this was making him look foolish and that he would do far better to make a classy exit. His last year was a time of some frustration for him (we did not pick his desired candidate to replace him) and for us, but it was also a time of celebration of his achievements, and I truly feel that by the end, we all felt good about how it all ended up."

The events leading up to Jesse's retirement from his organization constitute a success story even though there were plenty of bumps in the road. Many boards do not have the talent or the courage to manage such a transition, and the saddest stories are those in which the board does nothing, and an executive director who should depart is allowed to stay. The executive director can frighten the board into doing nothing by mustering supporters and threatening legal action. Cool heads are required on the board side that can persuade the incumbent of how much he or she has to lose by pursuing vindictive actions and how much he or she has to gain by cooperating.

In these very difficult situations, some trustees may grow angry and feel they owe the executive director nothing. But level heads can spell the difference between a very public and acrimonious parting, and one that is quiet and dignified. Even in cases where trustees need to bite their tongues and provide public accolades, the effort is usually well worth it.

Questions

1. Is the executive director's job description up-to-date? Does it spell out job responsibilities and expectations?
2. What is the process by which the executive director is reviewed by the board? Does it occur at least annually? Are job expectations set out for the coming year?
3. Is there a personnel manual that spells out the procedures for dismissal? If not, is there some other official document where this process is spelled out?
4. In addition to illegal activity, are there documented areas and policies that spell out activities that are grounds for dismissal?
5. Is the board prepared to have a conversation about when it may be time for a long-time executive director to move on?
6. What incentives can the board offer an executive director for a quiet, orderly resignation, and what will it expect in return?

14

GETTING HELP

In assessing the partnership between executive directors and boards, it is all too easy to cast it either in black or white—either the relationship is terrific or it is awful. But more often than not, it is more nuanced. True, in some organizations, everything is wonderful—just like a dream marriage. In others, it is so bad that the only solution is to part ways—a divorce of sorts. But, if it is true that most marriages are neither perfect on the one hand nor impossible on the other, the same is true for the relationship between an executive director and a board. And like in a marriage, sometimes the best solution for a relationship problem is to call in outside help.

Identifying the fact that there is a problem is the first step toward solving it. While many may experience discomfort with the situation, even discussing it among themselves, it is better if there is an internal process that is more rigorous and objective. The executive director's annual performance review offers one such opportunity. Generally carried out between the board president and the executive director, it should give all board members an opportunity to weigh in and the executive director a chance to express his or her views on how the relationship with the board is working. In one such process, the board president will circulate a questionnaire that allows trustees to rate the executive director on many dimensions—often taken right from the job description—and also allows them to write more extended prose describing their responses. These are synthesized and shared with the executive director, and further action can be agreed upon after a response is received and assessed.

At times, additional reviews may be scheduled, especially if something comes up during the year that has to be addressed. Often, agreement on changed behavior, either on the part of the executive director or the board or both, is discussed, agreed to, and memorialized in writing for the personnel file. At times, if the situation merits it, the executive director is put on probation, with specific performance objectives to be achieved within a circumscribed period of time.

Sometimes, however, the situation calls for a different approach. Many executive directors' problems are not something they can fix on their own without help. Neither carrots nor sticks are sufficient. What is needed is some instruction and guidance. In these cases, an outside resource person can diffuse a situation and lead everyone to a more harmonious working situation.

Boris was the executive director of a nonprofit organization that provided theatrical performances throughout the summer to tens of thousands of people in seven states. Generally, Boris was the model executive director. He had been with his organization for almost a decade, and as one board member put it, "like an old shoe, he fit well." He presided over a $2 million budget, a full-time staff of ten, and a seasonal staff of over seventy who carried out the various summer activities. With so many individuals under his jurisdiction spread over such a large geographic area, and with many of them moving from one location to another, Boris, and the board, felt it was imperative to develop detailed personnel policies that ensured the employees knew where they stood and the organization was protected. The completion of the personnel manual was an accomplishment much celebrated by board and staff.

But there was another reason why the personnel manual was important. Boris was often not a good supervisor, and the board thought that providing him with a kind of guidebook with documented policies might help. He was often too busy to give explicit instructions to those he supervised, and then he was impatient when employees didn't seem to understand what he wanted. Most could deal with his idiosyncrasies—"Boris is just being Boris," they joked. But for one employee, it was no joking matter. Boris and Joan had an increasingly toxic working relationship.

Boris's side of the story was that Joan just wouldn't follow directions and always made excuses. Often, when he asked her why a particular task had not been completed, she would tell him that she had done exactly what he had asked, but that those instructions had been garbled and confusing. "If you didn't get what you wanted, it is not my fault." In other cases, she said that the task had been unreasonable, impossible to accomplish in the time allotted. On some occasions, Boris would get angry, setting off Joan, who would return to her office, and according to Boris, "throw a tantrum, upsetting her colleagues."

Finally, it just became too much for Boris. Joan made what he considered a lame excuse one time too many. He lost his temper and fired Joan on the spot, telling her to take her things and go. The next day, Boris had the bookkeeper mail Joan her check for back pay (including unused vacation time), plus another to cover two weeks of severance, even though it was unclear from the personnel manual whether this was required, since he felt he had fired her "for cause." Also included was a letter confirming that Joan was no longer employed by the organization. Boris called the president of the board and told her what had happened. "I didn't handle it well," Boris conceded. "I hope Joan doesn't complain to one of our funders or to the state."

There was much concern on the part of the board. As much as they liked Boris, this had not been the first time there had been such difficulties, though it was by far the worst. The annual personnel evaluation just a few months earlier had addressed the issue, and Boris promised to improve. But concern mounted even further when a week later a group of employees approached the board president expressing their upset over the incident. "This is awkward," they conceded. "We know we are not supposed to approach the board directly. But Boris is our supervisor, and he is the problem." It was not necessarily that they did not agree with the decision, they said, but personnel procedures had not been followed. What good was a personnel manual if the executive director could ignore it, especially one like Boris who had a temper problem?

The board was fond of Boris. They admired his accomplishments. But he clearly had a problem. He was going to need help. After much discussion, they decided that putting Boris on probation was not the right move. They asked him whether he would agree to work with an executive coach who could help work through the problem. When Boris agreed, the staff was informed and told that they would be asked to help solve the problem by providing confidential opinions about Boris and about their working relationship with him to the coach. They were assured that their jobs would not be in jeopardy. They should be frank and the more honest they were, the sooner the problem would get fixed.

The executive coach conducted the interviews and subsequently worked with Boris to come up with a plan to address his weaknesses. The most significant step, readily agreed to by the board, was the creation of a new staff position, a managing director, to ease the pressure on Boris and to allow him to focus on what he did best. Though Boris himself would be doing the hiring of this new person, the coach would help him identify someone with the right set of skills.

Part of the process of working through the issues was getting Boris to acknowledge the consequences and potential consequences of his actions. He had upset his staff. He had wasted a great deal of board and staff time for what in the end he described as "my childishness." More importantly, he had never thought about all the ramifications of his actions. Joan could have taken the organization to court and possibly won a judgment, or at the very least, cost the organization lots of money and time in legal fees. She could have bad-mouthed the organization to funders she knew. The fact that she didn't wasn't the point. Boris had put the organization at risk.

Later, a meeting was called at which senior staff reporting to Boris, key trustees, and Boris himself met to discuss the plan, with the coach serving as mediator. The result was that everyone felt that the problem had been addressed, relationships were strengthened, and the organization could get back to its core business. Boris continued to meet with the coach for a few weeks thereafter as things continued to improve.

There are other situations where an executive director may need some assistance, not because of a problematic behavior, but simply due to lack of experience. This can occur when an individual is hired for a position with strong program knowledge and skills, but fewer strengths in administration or fundraising areas. A board may determine that the strengths of the individual far outweigh the weaknesses, but addressing the latter is essential if the individual is going to succeed. Getting the individual to acknowledge the areas of weakness is a first step. Getting him or her to seek help is often the greater challenge. Yet boards should insist on such action when a formal evaluation reveals weaknesses. It is in everyone's best interest to address a problem before it becomes so serious that more draconian actions are called for.

Mel had been an academic superstar before becoming executive director of one of the leading (and largest) humanities organizations in the United States. With an endowment of half a billion dollars and a staff of over a hundred, the organization had enjoyed stable and distinguished leadership for almost a hundred years, though most of Mel's predecessors had come to the executive director job late in their careers. Mel, at just over forty, was cut out of different cloth. He brought youth, energy, and new ideas. His interview had stunned the search committee, who found Mel brilliant, personable, and full of inspiration about new directions.

Mel knew that the job of executive director in a major nonprofit would be a stretch, and so did his board. But he was confident that he could learn quickly, and he was hired despite a lack of administrative experience. Some board members expressed concern, but others pointed out that there were several deputy directors in the organization who could provide support in finance, fundraising, and human resources, and members of the board could provide feedback and counsel when needed. The trustees had wanted a fresh face that could attract a younger generation of visitors and supporters and could address, in an innovative way, some of the challenges facing the humanities in the twenty-first century.

By and large, Mel's first year was successful. He was a quick study. He diagnosed strengths and weaknesses with the objective eye of an outsider, without offending long-time staff and trustees. He was able to propose major new initiatives that were exciting and transformative. New donors came into the fold.

Many of the skills that he had lacked he learned very quickly to the delight of the board.

But there was a problem. Mel still had many administrative skills to learn. Indeed, some were advising him to go to business school part-time to gain them. Furthermore, there was another problem, this one a bit more subtle. Mel had worked in an academic setting for all of his professional life, where individual achievement was the coin of the realm. Being the smartest guy in the room was a sign of being the best. But in a nonprofit setting, Mel needed to build a team, and taking credit for being smart and the guy with the best ideas did not tend to foster that kind of congeniality and teamwork.

Mel and his board agreed that some executive coaching would be appropriate. The program Mel chose involved questionnaires being sent to colleagues, board members, and constituents who rated Mel across several dimensions. In a very short time, Mel and his coach had identified strengths (of which there were many) and weaknesses on which he was to work. Within six months, there was widespread agreement that Mel was a new person, a superb leader, and a team player.

Questions

1. Is there a regular system in place for identifying problems in the relationship between the board and executive director? If not, how can the problem be addressed?

2. Can this system also pick out shortcomings in the relationship between the board and the executive director? If not, how can that challenge be addressed?

3. What diagnostic tools are available for pinpointing problems in the performance of the executive director? Are there triggers that lead to the scheduling of special sessions if they cannot wait for regularly scheduled performance evaluations?

4. What various actions are possible when problems are identified with the executive director's performance? Who is responsible for working out the steps with the executive director that can lead to improved performance?

5. What kinds of outside assistance might be appropriate to help an executive director improve performance? Is the board prepared to pay to secure this kind of help?

6. How might the board or the staff or both be productively drawn into the executive director counseling process?

15

BAD NEWS . . . AND GOOD

S hould a nonprofit organization have an official spokesperson? Should there be an individual authorized to speak for an organization publicly and officially when there is important information to convey? How should the organization deal with the media in these situations? Who should be in charge of crafting the message when a lot is at stake? What kind of internal communication mechanisms are there when the board and the staff need to be informed quickly of the content of an important information release, and what are the protocols for answering questions, if asked? And most importantly, how can the board and executive director work out the rules for all these things ahead of time so events proceed smoothly when the pressure is on?

Most of these questions can be answered in a board-approved communications plan for the board and staff (and sometimes volunteers) that establishes policies in this area and is periodically reviewed and updated. Even in organizations with relatively small boards and staffs, this can be an important tool. There is always a danger that important information will be communicated in different ways by different people. Much of the time, this doesn't matter. Trustees and staff are expected to engage in conversations about the organization all the time, and there is no way that each will say the same thing in the same way about a particular topic. In most cases, that is a good thing. The role of trustees includes being enthusiastic promoters of an organization's work, and the fact that each person has a unique take on things and a specific way of talking about it is part of the authenticity of the message. Staff members, too, need to talk about the organization as part of their jobs. They must answer questions and discuss activities regularly, and each will have different things to convey and to emphasize. There is no upside to a communication straitjacket in nonprofit organizations, and those who try to impose them generally do a disservice. On the other hand, people must be aware and ready when discipline is required. They need to know when a topic is off limits, when a message needs to be carefully crafted, and when it should be delivered through a single spokesperson.

Here are some guidelines:

- First, detailed financial and personnel information may not be openly discussed with outsiders unless officially authorized.
- Second, any on-the-record communication with the media must be authorized and carefully planned. Off-the-record conversations should not be permitted.
- Third, any major news about the organization—pro or con—should be delivered first by an official spokesperson and then by others in a manner consistent with the original message.
- Finally, in a crisis, there needs to be a group that can be assembled quickly to craft a message and a single individual who will deliver it. All questions must be directed to this individual. Unless one of them is implicated, the spokesperson should most frequently be the executive director, though in certain cases, it may be the board president.

Dave had had a successful career as a fundraiser when he was picked as executive director for a local United Way organization.

His work was challenging—raising money generally is—but it was also rewarding, and the new job gave Dave the opportunity to talk with community leaders and contributors. For several years, Dave thrived and never experienced a problem that he couldn't handle with his experience, competence, and winning personality.

Then a major crisis almost derailed Dave's career. Like others who worked for United Way at the time, he had to deal with news that had the potential to turn him into a pariah. "Imagine trying to look a donor in the face when your national CEO is going to prison for fraud," he recalled. The William Aramony scandal may be in the far-distant past and largely forgotten, but for Dave, it seems like yesterday. "Having to answer angry accusations about charitable dollars being diverted to expensive vacations for Aramony and his mistress was not something I would want to have to go through again. But it taught me about how to deal with a crisis. And all I can say is: You had better have a committed and courageous board. When the bad news hit, our executive committee called an emergency meeting, and we came up with a plan of what to say, who would say it, and how to move on. Had the president of my board not stepped forward, I don't think I could have handled it, and I might not have survived in my position. Yet, because of his credibility and steadfastness, we met the challenge and even achieved our fundraising goals that year."

Dave was fortunate his board president was a corporate CEO who knew from his day job that any major corporation has to have a plan for communicating with the public when things go awry. Good CEOs are trained to know what to do. They stay calm, have a spokesperson, and stick to a script. In Dave's organization's case, the script was simple: "We are an independent organization; while we are a local affiliate of a national organization, we are completely independent of any wrongdoing, and we are the same successful community resource that people have known and supported for decades." Dave's board president repeated the information over and over again. And soon Dave was authorized to take interviews and repeat it.

More recently, Dave was tested again. This time, the potential crisis was anticipated and dealt with before it even materialized. Dave had moved on and was now the executive director of another funding entity that distributed local donations to social service organizations. When Dave took over, he realized there were some problems with the distribution policies—who was getting the money that was raised and who wasn't. It wasn't that anything illegal or untoward was going on. But a few organizations were receiving the lion's share of the money and were pretty much guaranteed support because of historical precedent; meanwhile, lots of newer ones could not gain access to the "club." Dave and his board wanted to address this situation and take on new initiatives, even perhaps partnering with the grantees on special projects. But because so much of the money was going to these organizations with practically no strings attached, there was no way to direct the money to major community priorities. Many of Dave's contributors were beginning to question their support.

Dave met quietly with his board. A small committee was formed to look into the matter and report back. While most agreed that the funding policies had to change, the greatest worry was the fallout that would occur when the grantees heard the bad news. "The last thing we wanted was public controversy as we were about to gear up our fundraising campaign for the year, and there was definitely that possibility. While some of our donors were going to be pleased if we changed our funding policies, others associated with the major recipient organizations that would be losing money were fiercely partisan to the old system. Crafting the bad news message was going to be important. Delivering it effectively would be crucial."

Once again, Dave was fortunate in his board. "We agreed from the outset that the news could not be leaked, and amazingly, even with a twenty-five-member board, it wasn't. We also agreed that in fairness, we needed to let the grantees know first, but within minutes afterwards, we needed to be on the phone with some of their (and our) staunchest supporters. Patricia, our president, was going to be our chief spokesperson, and I was also going to be available to answer questions. But the entire board was primed with the message so trustees wouldn't be caught flat-footed if confronted. When the news hit and the questions came, we were ready. We may have been overprepared. We were actually surprised that the fallout was so manageable."

Sometimes, bad news is so egregious that there is no spokesperson in the organization left with sufficient credibility to convey the message. Indeed, there are times when an orderly transition to new leadership (both executive and board) is the only thing that will suffice. In these extreme situations, the board president will generally convey the initial message, announcing the changes, and at the same time, designate the new leader who has sufficient credibility to communicate with the public going forward.

An academic organization with a history going back 150 years found itself in the news . . . but not in a way it might have hoped. The executive director had faked his resumé, and his academic credentials were bogus. Nor was this something that had been discovered internally and addressed by the board. It had been ferreted out by a reporter and was soon going viral through the media and on the Internet. The board was caught completely by surprise.

The storied membership of the organization was in shock, but the problems did not end with the inflated qualifications.

The executive director's salary, it turned out, was totally out of line with what might be considered appropriate, coming in-between 40 percent and 80 percent higher than what experts felt were comparable positions. Furthermore, some staff members took out their long-time frustrations with the executive director—frustrations never dealt with by the board—and began a public whistle-blowing campaign that was played out day after day in excruciating detail.

Under the circumstances, it was clear that the executive director had to go. But what about the board? Clearly, the board had fallen down in its responsibilities, both in initially retaining an unqualified executive leader, and subsequently in not guiding and supervising him. The trustees had not carefully checked his resumé initially, had approved and increased an inflated salary, and had not ensured that internal operations were proceeding satisfactorily.

Within a week, the board president announced the departure of the executive director, as well as his own decision to step down. A new leader—with a storied national reputation—had agreed to step in and promised complete transparency as the organization sought new executive leadership, underwent a governance review, and studied the internal systems that led to the breakdown. Other trustees agreed to tender their resignations as soon as suitable replacements could be found.

The examples cited above were situations of extreme public embarrassment for the organizations and the people responsible for leading them. The bad news was very bad news. Sometimes, however, bad news is much less unsettling and may involve simply telling someone something he or she doesn't want to hear. For an executive director or a member of the board, this can be delicate and even awkward. Suppose a funder wants to see a change in the way a program is delivered, or a valued supporter of the organization is pushing a friend or relative to fill a staff vacancy. What if a staff person is looking for a big increase in his or her discretionary budget or a salary increase? It may be difficult to say "no" outright without at least temporarily undermining a close working relationship or continued support. In these cases, the board can be a great help in an uncannily simple way. The words, "I will get back to you after I check with the trustees," are some of the most useful in the executive director's arsenal and can also be useful for board members caught in uncomfortable situations.

The fact that the board can be used as a reason to defer a decision (and then make one that will make the listener unhappy) makes it more likely that a positive relationship can be retained. The board is an amorphous group whose decision-making structure is more opaque. In many cases, an executive director may not actually "check with the board," but may simply mention the conversation in passing to the president or to another board member if there is any concern that anyone might check to see whether the topic had been discussed. But often, just letting time go by before passing on the disappointing news, "Sorry, but I just don't think it will fly" is sufficient, and gives the listener the satisfaction of knowing that the request was not rejected out of hand.

With so much focus on how to deliver bad news, it is worth mentioning the importance of good news and thinking about who should get the opportunity to deliver it. Here some selflessness on the part of an executive director can cement good feelings with the board. It is good to remember that serving on a nonprofit board involves giving time and money, solving thorny problems, and unlike the executive director, not going home with a paycheck. The pleasure that comes from being an organizational spokesperson when things go well is obvious, and if trustees often have to take the slings and arrows and the anxieties and sacrifices that come with board service, then they need to be given some of the fun as well.

Beyond announcements and press briefings, a board president or another member of the board may well take on the task of addressing the local chamber of commerce, the Rotary, or the school board.

Properly scripted, with perhaps a PowerPoint presentation, this gives these individuals a real opportunity to shine. Indeed, one of Dave's trustees, who was thinking about running for the local school board, was given the opportunity to make a presentation at the annual meeting of the parent-teacher organization. And when the organization later won a national award for its education initiative, it was that same trustee who was featured in the photograph that got in the local newspaper. Dave considered it one of the rewards for board service.

Questions

1. Does the organization have a formal communications plan, including a plan for crisis communications as well as for good news, that is shared with the board?

2. Are there guidelines for selecting the official spokesperson for the organization? Are there situations where it could be more than one person?

3. What constitutes information that should only go through official channels in order to be properly communicated to the community? On other matters, if the board or staff is called for comment, what is the policy with regard to their permission to provide information?

4. Is there a crisis protocol to ensure that a message will be crafted quickly, the board and staff notified, and a single individual ready to step forward as the message point person?

5. Are people sufficiently aware of the possibility of deferring awkward decisions by invoking the need to consult with the board? What is the follow-through and board-notification process when this occurs?

6. Has sufficient thought been given to how good news is delivered to the community? Are board members selected for this task? Are there public speaking opportunities where board members can be given a chance to shine?

16

OH NO, NOT ANOTHER MEETING

How does one design and carry out successful board meetings in nonprofit organizations, and what are the elements of a successful meeting? A partial list might include:

- Having stimulating, meaningful, and important items on an agenda that will lead to critical issues getting resolved.
- Ensuring that proper background information is sent out sufficiently ahead of time and that trustees can review it before the meetings, so that time will not be wasted on reading reports or other routine material in the meeting.
- Limiting the time of the business meeting so that people are not discouraged from attending or leave before the meeting is over.
- Sticking to a timetable for action items (those that need to be decided by a vote), and tabling issues that cannot be resolved within a reasonable time.
- Preventing surprises and unbridled controversy.
- Giving people other incentives to attend, including a nice space, food, stimulating and important topics that will contribute to

trustee learning, and time in advance or after the meeting for social interaction.

Many trustees complain about the dispiriting feeling that comes after attending unsuccessful board meetings. What makes the meetings so bad? Meetings can be too long. They can be too short, without adequate time to complete the agenda. They can be full of controversy, or on the other hand, they can have absolutely nothing of importance on the agenda and be simply *pro forma*. They can fail to resolve important issues or resolve and vote on them so quickly that some trustees feel they were ignored. They can be dominated by too few people, or they can seem to lack a strong leader who keeps them under control. They can make people feel as if they have wasted their time, or because of poor advance notice, they can make others feel they missed something important through no fault of their own. To paraphrase Tolstoy, each unhappy board meeting is unhappy in its own way.

Part of the problem is that there are many misconceptions about board meetings:

- First, some people believe that all important decisions need to be made at a board meeting. In fact, many decisions can be made by staff or by an executive committee where one exists. Knowing what rises to the level of full board purview is something that gradually has to be worked out in every organization, but the emphasis should always be first on legal, financial, and policy decisions.

- Second, those less experienced with effective board meetings come prepared to discuss and debate. But this is not the primary purpose of the meeting. It is to make decisions. Issues should be extensively discussed in other forums, like committee meetings. By the time a decision comes before the board, most of the wrinkles should be ironed out.

- Another misconception is that as organizations grow, board meetings need to become longer. In fact, successful meetings of large organizations are often some of the shortest, given the busy schedules of the trustees. Much time should be spent carefully prioritizing and structuring an agenda.

- Some believe that a board meeting is an appropriate time to find out how trustees feel about action items (those that will be voted on at the meeting). But this is a recipe for problems. If there is not a fairly good idea of how action items on the agenda will be decided, they should not be on the agenda in the first place.

- Finally, many board members and executive directors are under the impression that planning board meetings is the exclusive province of the trustees. In fact, successful meetings are developed in a partnership of the board leadership and the executive director, often with much of the design being worked out in an executive committee meeting at which the executive director is present.

Sally was a first-time executive director at a small nonprofit organization. She was relatively young, and due to her lack of experience, she felt she should be deferential to her board. When it came to board meetings, she attended only when invited, and her only involvement in meeting planning was planning the refreshments. Meetings themselves were often excruciating, and she always obsessed about them for days in advance. She would receive the agendas and worry how the votes would go. Often in the meetings, discussion was extended and contentious, and sometimes an item would have to be tabled, as some trustees left the meeting early, and there was no longer a quorum for a legal vote. After the meetings ended, the president would invite any trustees who remained to go out for dinner and leave the controversy behind. Sally was invited to these dinners, but was often too upset to eat.

It was in her second job as executive director that Sally gained some perspective and knowledge. This board president was an older, experienced trustee, and they consulted regularly. He told Sally she was always expected at board meetings unless the group went into executive session, which they rarely did. He believed in focusing the board on the things that, as he put it, were "under our purview," and leaving to the staff those decisions that were more of an everyday nature. "Boards spend entirely too much time getting into the nitty-gritty. It is not their job. We have legal and fiduciary responsibilities, and we need to focus there first. Then we need to develop policy and think about the long-term future. We are not here to design programs."

At first, Sally was concerned that if too much was left to the staff, there would be inadequate trustee involvement and buy-in, and a lack of knowledge or commitment. This turned out not to be the case. Ed, the board president, believed that trustees should be deeply involved where they had an interest and were willing to spend time, but that this should happen at the committee level and with the guidance of the staff. "Committees are where the real work will get done, and by having trustees involved, the board will feel reassured that the staff is not going off half-cocked. When something comes up for full board approval, it should often be at the recommendation of a committee, and the committee chair should, in most cases, make the motion."

But trustee approval, it turned out, could happen at two levels. In this organization, with its robust committee structure, all committees shared their work with a coordinating body—the executive committee—that, in turn, was empowered to approve their work without it needing to come before the full board for a vote. When the executive committee felt a case to be sufficiently important, they would make a recommendation to place the item on the full board agenda. "By the time something gets to the full board," Ed pointed out, "it will have gone through two reviews and have a group of trustees ready to fight for it, if necessary. But I would never put anything on the agenda for a decision that was going to be controversial, anyway. I would always test the waters first. Board meetings are not the place for divisive discussions about items on which we are to vote."

As Sally and Ed continued their work together, she was amazed at how smoothly things went. Admittedly, the process was time-consuming. But board meetings were a breeze, and they always seemed to end when Ed's agenda said they would. She asked him how he knew how long a board meeting should be. "Like my college professor used to say when people asked him how long the term paper should be," he said, "long enough to cover the subject, but not so long as to be boring. And frankly, any meeting longer than ninety minutes is boring by definition."

In Sally's earliest board meetings—the ones she dreaded—she noticed that a few people did most of the talking. That included her, since as executive director, she was the one who had most of the facts at her fingertips. Often, she could sense that some people were bored. One of her trustees regularly drifted off to sleep. Ed's meetings were magical by comparison. Everyone participated, and he would often ignore someone's raised hand in discussion in order to pick someone else who had been silent. Strangely, it did not seem to matter. The crucial information got shared.

Ed explained it this way. "I think of every board member who is attending as someone who should be heard at some point in the meeting. I know what their areas of interest are, so I know when to call on them. If things will require a more extensive presentation, I call trustees in advance and prepare them for the fact that I will be relying on them at a certain point in the meeting. They tend to stay more alert throughout the meeting that way. Some are responsible for presenting an entire agenda item. Others give a progress report on something that relates to an item we are discussing. I always consider it a failure if there is someone who has not said anything. Remember, as executive director and board president, you and I look good to the extent we get what we want without having to plead for it. Our silence should reflect confidence in the process."

At least one major nonprofit organization—one composed of very busy trustees—has an innovative way of handling its board meetings. They are strictly divided into two parts. Trustees take care of all-important current business in the first hour (which sometimes includes a report from a staff person about an existing program or initiative). Then they break for lunch. At lunch, they generally invite a distinguished speaker to come talk to them about a mission-related topic, one that touches on important trends that will affect the organization's future, or examples of best-practices from elsewhere. The talk is about fifteen to twenty minutes, with an equal amount of time for questions and discussions. Attendance at lunch is optional but is remarkably good. The opportunity to have mission-related and even controversial conversation is important, but it should be set up in a way that respects the time constraints of busy people and does not subvert the need to make decisions in a timely manner.

Not every organization will be able to attract great speakers to every board meeting, nor should they try. This is the format that works for one particular organization. But three things should be noted:

- First, the board has time as a group to consider long-range issues—to learn about them and discuss them—outside of the business meeting and without the pressure of having to make decisions.
- Second, they have access to outside expertise.
- And third, the executive director and the board together establish the topics and the people who will help educate the board.

Those with experience in planning meetings of nonprofit boards make three other suggestions:

- First, an executive session is a portion of the board meeting where trustees can speak candidly without others present (like staff and guests). Some boards only include these on the agenda when there is a burning issue that needs to be discussed privately. This can cause some anxiety on the part of the staff, since on many occasions the discussion items can involve personnel issues. For this reason, and because it is useful to be able to have a candid discussion at any time, other organizations always place an executive session at the end of each board meeting agenda, so as not to draw special attention to it at specific times. One function of these sessions can be some kind of self-evaluation—an opportunity for the board to reflect on how it is doing, whether the meeting format is working well, how effectively skills and expertise are being used. On the other hand, if there is no business to discuss, the executive session can be rapidly adjourned.

- Second, at least once a year, the board should hold a retreat to look at longer-term, mission-related issues and to discuss the future. Once again, the board and the executive director will generally plan these sessions together, sometimes with the assistance of an outside facilitator.

- Finally it is good to remember that one of the benefits of trusteeship is the possibility of social engagement among interesting people. There should always be some time either prior to the meeting or after, often with refreshments, when people who wish to can talk informally. Such opportunities can be enriched by inviting staff.

Questions

1. Are board meetings carefully planned with meaningful and important agenda items that can be decided without undue controversy?

2. Is there a committee system that allows detailed and controversial information to be discussed and vetted in advance by selected trustees and staff, so they are able to come before the full board with committee endorsement?

3. Is material sent out in advance so that routine or detailed information does not have to take up valuable board-meeting time?

4. How well do the executive director and the executive committee work together to ensure that board meetings focus on the important issues?

5. Is there a mechanism to determine how votes will go before meetings take place? Is the president prepared to turn an action item into a discussion item if decisions cannot be reached in the allotted time?

6. How often does the board convene to discuss longer-range and controversial issues? Is the executive director properly utilized in planning these meetings? Are outside resource people used? Are these sessions clearly differentiated from business meetings?

17

HOW MANY BOARDS
DO WE HAVE?

This book has focused on the relationship between an executive director and a board in nonprofit organizations. Making this relationship productive and positive has its challenges, as we have seen. But imagine a situation where the relationship is not between two parties, but between three or more. Some executive directors have to work with two boards (and sometimes with a third party unattached to either board who serves as the executive director's supervisor).

These situations occur frequently enough that it is important to review how they come about. In one model, a large nonprofit organization may have a divisional structure with different units. At the top of the hierarchy, there is a board and staff head who oversee and administer the entire system. In addition, each division has its own semiautonomous board and executive director. Because these divisional executive directors have their own self-contained units, including a staff they supervise and a board they report to, they function most of the time as though they were running an independent nonprofit organization. However, they will ultimately be accountable to two boards, and to complicate matters, it is often the overall system staff head who has ultimate authority over their continued tenure in their positions.

Jim was the executive director of the New York–based division of his nonprofit international aid organization. An experienced professional who had worked overseas on three continents, he was respected for his experience and knowledge and his ability to raise money. When originally offered the job, he was skeptical. The parent organization was incorporated in the United States as a 501(c)(3) nonprofit corporation, based in Chicago with a national board. At the local level, each division had its own board to which was delegated partial governance responsibility (e.g., it was the local board that hired Jim). On the other hand, major policy decisions were made nationally.

Jim's original caution turned out to be unfounded. In his ten years with the organization, Jim never had a problem with the dual board structure. Each of the six division boards had a president who served on the national board, and there was ongoing communication about matters of mutual interest and concern. The national organization had established clear standards and requirements that divisions had to meet each year (as an example, divisions could not run at a deficit unless expressly released from this requirement in any particular year). So long as divisions met the standards and requirements, the national board did not meddle.

Jim realized there was much that was beneficial about the structure. The national organization worked hard to promote the brand, and the organization was widely known and admired. It entered into national funding agreements at a scale that no divisions could hope to achieve, and the divisions benefited directly. Finally, the national organization provided technical assistance; a national conference; advice; a purchasing pool for discounted equipment, supplies, and insurance; and many other advantages. Jim wondered why more organizations didn't utilize the system, though he was the first to acknowledge that the potential for problems was always present.

There are other situations of multiple boards that differ from what Jim experienced. A common one arises when a nonprofit entity is part of the public sector—that is, it is legally part of government. Think of a state college or a public hospital, library, or museum. Most of these organizations will depend in part on private sector contributions, and since donors generally shy away from giving their contributions to government, there is often an affiliated, private nonprofit organization with its own board, and sometimes with its own staff, to handle the fundraising. Often, too, if there is an endowment, the private sector organization holds and manages it.

These public-private hybrids come in many forms. On the public side, one model is for the entity to be part of a department or division of government that, in turn, has legal and fiduciary oversight responsibility. The executive director in these cases is a public employee, reporting to a supervisor who also is part of the governmental system (like an agency director, a division head, or a city manager). In other situations, the public entity may be a semi-independent public trust or other semiautonomous unit with its own board, often appointed by public officials, that has the power to select, supervise, and dismiss the executive director. In still other cases, there is a mix of the two models: the executive director reports both to the public supervisor and to the public board.

As if this is not confusing enough, we now add the private nonprofit support organization. Government entities, for the most part, do not engage in private sector fundraising. So, a support organization, a 501(c)(3) nonprofit corporation, is created that is entirely independent of government. It has its own board, and in some cases, its own fundraising staff. The executive director can, in some cases, work for the private organization and be directly accountable to its board, while still reporting on the public side. In other cases, the executive director is not legally connected to the private organization.

But because that organization is there to raise money on behalf of the public entity, there needs to be a close working relationship between the executive director and the nonprofit corporation's board, and if there is one, its staff.

All this can be very bewildering and lead to confusion, overlapping areas of responsibility, and unclear lines of accountability. For the executive director, it can be fraught with uncertainty about who, ultimately, gets to make which decisions.

Robert, an experienced administrator who had run nonprofit theaters all over the United States, was hired by a large performing arts center. The center was originally built, and subsequently owned and operated, by the local municipality. When Robert was interviewed, he met with both the publicly appointed board of the center (each member of which was appointed by a city council member) and with the city manager. It was made clear to Robert that as a public sector employee, the city manager would be his supervisor, but that for the most part, when it came to programmatic decisions, he would be working for the public board. In addition, the performing arts center had an affiliated "foundation" with its own private board and fundraising staff whose purpose was to raise private sector funds. It also held and managed the center's endowment. The organization was a traditional 501(c)(3) nonprofit corporation with a board nominated and elected by its own members for set terms. While the private nonprofit entity had no authority over Robert's hiring, he was asked to interview with that board anyway as a courtesy. He also met with the private organization's staff even though, again, they were completely independent of his authority and chain of command.

Almost immediately upon taking the job, Robert encountered problems. The first had to do with developing the annual budget. While his public board had a finance committee that played a major role in helping him set priorities for projected revenues and expenses for the coming year, the city had its own budgeting process, which included working with the city's finance director and using a city budgeting protocol that was completely different from the one that had been set up for the center. The city's budget process also came with certain mandates, one of which was a required 5 percent cut in the personnel budget for the coming year, given the city's budget shortfall.

Robert was very concerned about the personnel issue. His staffing was already very thin, and no one had had a raise for two years. Working with his public board and with its concurrence, he proposed a budget in which increased private fundraising could make up the difference between what the city was allowing for staff salaries and benefits and what the center wished to pay. But the solution was short-lived. Robert was told by the budget director that the policy as developed required all city departments to make the mandated cuts, and that if the center felt it could raise additional money, then perhaps it did not need as many city dollars as had been budgeted. After a series of meetings in which board members argued for allowing the increase in the budget projection, the budget director said she would take the request under advisement and find out whether an exception could be made and staff levels could be maintained with private sector funds.

Having made progress with the budget director, Robert now ran into a new problem. He was encountering resistance from the private sector support organization's board. How dare he promise that cuts could be made up with more vigorous private sector fundraising without consulting with its leadership? How could his public board go ahead and approve a budget that required additional private dollars before the private organization had authorized the increase in its subsidy? Robert quickly learned that his authority and that of his public board to establish private sector fundraising goals was limited. He would have to make a case for the need and convince the staff of the nonprofit, who themselves were not enthusiastic about a large increase in their dollar goal in a recessionary climate. Meanwhile, the deadline for the city budget submission was only days away.

An emergency board meeting of the nonprofit was set in order to make a decision prior to the city's budgeting deadline. After much discussion, a fundraising goal was set for the year. Clearly, it would not be high enough to make up for cuts in the center's personnel budget. The public sector board members were furious. How could they do their job running the center if the private board was undermining them and refusing to raise adequate funds? The private sector board was equally upset. Since none of the public sector board members did any of the fundraising, and most of them did not contribute any money personally, what right had they to complain? Meanwhile, Robert was shuttling back and forth between city staff, public sector board, and private sector board, trying to maintain his work force for the coming year, submit a viable and acceptable budget, and run the center at the same time.

The problem Robert had run into was a structural one, and in the end, the solution, though not perfect, involved some changes in structure. It had been clear that there was a lack of communication between the two boards and unrealistic expectations of the proper role that each should play. One simple solution was to change statutes and bylaws such that the president and treasurer of each board were, *ex officio*, also members of the other board. While this doubled their workload and the number of meetings they needed to attend, it greatly reduced the time spent on trying to resolve problems of miscommunication and misunderstanding.

Multiple boards, staffs, and supervisors not only can provide difficult challenges to an executive director, but they can be problems for one another. Analyzing precisely what pressures operated on each, in the case of Robert and the performing arts center, may suggest how compromises can be orchestrated:

- The public sector budget director who was providing guidelines on what would be allowed in the financial presentation was not acting unilaterally and independently. Such guidelines are generally established either by a supervisor or someone even higher in the authority chain—elected officials, perhaps. The budget director may have had little room to maneuver and make exceptions. Understanding where there is flexibility is crucial, as is knowing where in the chain of command the ultimate decisions will be made.
- The public sector board believed, quite rightly, that if it had the responsibility for successfully overseeing the management of the center, it needed the appropriate tools. Having enough qualified staff was part of the requirement. So, too, was having adequate funds to pay them. Public sector board members felt it was perfectly reasonable to expect city officials to respond affirmatively to a solution that would address a staffing and budget problem and also believed that a private sector fundraising board should rise to the occasion and provide the funds necessary to do so.
- Private sector trustees were resentful that individuals who had no responsibility for fundraising were presuming to tell them how much they could and should raise. Their irritation was compounded by the fact that while they were being asked to give and get money, they had little to no authority over how the funds would be used, nor were they being asked to comment on how the center ought to be run, even though they were raising the private sector money for it. Some of them were saying that if others felt strongly that the fundraising goals were not high enough, then perhaps those individuals should help out by making personal contributions and finding new donors.
- Robert, the executive director, was in a particularly delicate position. The budget director who had set out the financial guidelines worked for the city manager to whom Robert also reported. Refusing to follow her directive without getting permission would be

considered a form of insubordination. The public sector board, while looking to support Robert, may, in fact, have made his position less tenable by insisting on a course that was not going to be acceptable, either to city staff or to the private sector board. At the same time, trying to convince the private sector board to raise its goals for fundraising was alienating the staff of that organization, individuals with whom Robert had to work, and its board.

Successful hybrid organizations are ones where effective communication helps everyone get ahead of problems before they are allowed to fester:

- Public sector board members must see their role in part as developing good working relationships with elected officials and senior staff, realizing that an executive director may have little or no authority to do so. They must keep communication channels open, making government officials aware of the challenges that the organization faces (and the good work it does to help realize community goals). They should learn about impending issues that will have an impact before these are translated into hard-and-fast policy decisions, since it is far easier to address an issue before it requires a request for reversing a decision already made. Public board members will often have direct access to the higher levels of power that the executive director cannot reach. They should use it when necessary.

- Public sector board members also must be sensitive to the pressures on their colleagues on the private side who do not want to be thought of only as money machines. They must feel part of the workings of the institution, their opinions on major policy and program issues should be sought, and they should be thanked routinely. It also helps if at least some of the public board members are themselves donors and are involved in fundraising activities.

- On the private side, it is essential that there is ongoing communication between the executive director and the private board and staff. Occasionally, the executive director may actually be a member of the private organization's staff in full or in part, but where that is not the case, the communication channels have to be regular and thorough.

- Consultation should not simply be about fundraising and budget issues, but also should include issues of interest in programming and administration. Successes and challenges should be discussed, so that there is strong institutional ownership on the private side and strong incentives to raise funds vigorously. In addition, where there are strong community leaders serving on the private board, they should be enlisted in the public advocacy work with city officials on behalf of friendly legislation, policy, and public funding.
- Of particular importance is cross membership on the two boards. The president of each board, at a minimum, should serve *ex officio* on the other board, and sometimes there should be more positions reserved on each board for members of the other. This ensures better communication and an ability to hear concerns that can be communicated back from the public side to the private side and vice versa, taking some pressure off the executive director to be the exclusive go between.
- Finally, there needs to be absolute clarity about the reporting chain for the executive director. Dual or even treble reports (in some organizations, the executive director reports to the public employee supervisor, the public board, and the private board) are fraught with danger. The executive director needs to know who in the end has the ultimate power to fire him or her (or whether it is a joint decision), and who sets expectations for the job and evaluates his or her performance. If there is shared responsibility, then the process of review has to be clear and transparent.

Before leaving the topic, it is important to acknowledge that, in addition to the two models of multiple board arrangements that have been mentioned, there are situations where one private nonprofit organization has another affiliated one, much like in the public-private hybrid already discussed. This is particularly common in cases where the second entity is responsible for oversight and administration of an endowment. This second organization generally has its own board, established to ensure independence, to manage the assets, and to prevent overspending (and overdrawing) by the main programming entity. In some cases, the second organization will also be a fund-raising entity, just as we saw in the public-private structure.

While the structure of two affiliated nonprofits is legally different from that of the public-private hybrid, many of the issues dealt with in the chapter are similar. The relationships must be maintained carefully through good communication, there needs to be mutual respect, and the executive director must be protected from unreasonable pulls in different directions by the two boards.

Questions

1. Is the organization a public or private sector entity? Is it part of a divisional structure with multiple boards? Does it have an independently linked, private nonprofit support organization with its own board?

2. Is the executive director a public or private employee, and to whom does he or she report? If there are multiple reports, is it clear who has ultimate authority over the executive director's continued tenure in the position?

3. Who evaluates the executive director? If there are multiple processes, are they coordinated?

4. If there are multiple boards, is there cross membership, such that public members serve on the private board, and vice versa? What other strategies are there for regular communication?

5. What is the budget process? Who is ultimately responsible for approving the budget? Are there ways that all parties can have input into the process?

6. How strong is communication between all parties? Is the private board in regular communication with public board members and the executive director? Are private board members party to important decisions outside of fundraising, even if they do not have voting privileges on such matters?

18

HOW MANY EXECUTIVE DIRECTORS DO WE HAVE?

The previous chapter dealt with the problem of multiple boards. This one deals with the challenge of multiple executive directors. How is such a situation possible? How can there be two people, both with full executive authority, dealing with what may be, or appears to be, the same organization? There are at least three different ways in which this can occur:

- In the first instance (and the one that is organizationally least complicated), a single nonprofit organization may have two individuals sharing executive director responsibilities who are considered coequals. This can be the result of a merger in which the executive directors of each of the two original organizations are retained, and both are given equivalent titles and authority in the merged entity. Alternatively, it can be the result of two individuals agreeing to share a single job. Or, it can come about because of a particular organizational philosophy of distributed leadership.

- In the second model, one that was profiled in detail in the previous chapter, two legally distinct organizational units share responsibility for a single entity, as in the case of a city's public library or a state college that has an attached, nonprofit fundraising organization.

Each unit (in this case, one publicly administered with government employees, and a second that is a private nonprofit with its own separate staff) may be led by its own executive director. While each of the units is legally independent, functionally they have overlapping missions and areas of focus. In some cases, they may even share a board.

- A third example occurs when the responsibilities of the top staff member are considered so extensive—and require such a broad range of skills—that they must be distributed among two individuals. Each party to the arrangement has his or her own jurisdiction of authority, but both report directly to the board and are coequal in terms of seniority and authority. Think of a hospital where there is both a medical director and an administrative director or a museum where there is someone in charge of administration and a coequal who is the curatorial head. The individuals may have different titles and their job descriptions may be different, but neither has authority over the other, and both are at the top of their respective staff hierarchies.

Each of these situations comes with its own set of challenges, but there are commonalities. Perhaps most fundamentally, no single person is ultimately in charge. Even in the case where the two job descriptions differ and there are apparently distinct jurisdictions of activity, both directors are regarded as "chiefs," and there is much potential for friction. As long as they agree, the organization can generally operate smoothly. But when they disagree, especially when the area of disagreement is in the grey zone between their areas of authority, there can be problems. The board (or in some cases, multiple boards) has to resolve the issues, a special challenge when the trustees themselves cannot agree.

Case histories involving single organizations with multiple executive directors running into problems are fairly common, and reviewing them suggests ways that the problems can be addressed.

Roger and Melinda were both executive directors of successful national youth service organizations supported by a national foundation. Both had founded their respective organizations as small local initiatives fostering youth development. Both designed programs that placed at-risk young people in community settings. With success, both saw their organizations grow to the point where they had regional and then national constituencies and programs. Both took on national advocacy as a prime responsibility and began to garner significant public funding. With time, the foundation officer responsible for core funding to their respective organizations felt there was simply too much duplication and encouraged the boards of the two organizations to discuss a merger. An additional one-time grant of a million dollars was dangled as an incentive to "cover the costs and dislocation" of a merger, if the two boards could agree on a course of action that turned two organizations into one.

The initial discussions went well, largely because Roger and Melinda embraced the concept of merger. The scenario they laid out would have both of them continuing as codirectors, with each bringing a specific set of skills and experiences to the venture. The two boards, thrilled that they could retain two field leaders, rapidly agreed to the plan, the merger was consummated, and the million dollars that the foundation granted was placed into an endowment.

Almost immediately, there were problems. Roger was often on the road, so Melinda was expected to make day-to-day decisions and deal with staff requests while he was away. Roger increasingly felt that Melinda was trying to usurp his authority, especially with those who had worked for him in his old organization. Roger, the fiscal conservative, would say no to a request for a particular expenditure from a staff member, depart on a trip, then realize Melinda had authorized it while he was away. Increasingly, as executive committee meetings and other board committee meetings would get scheduled, it was Melinda whose availability was sought, and Roger felt he was being intentionally excluded. He demanded that no major meetings be held unless he was in town, which incurred the ire of several trustees, whose own schedules were tight.

As things began to deteriorate, Roger complained to some of his original board members and Melinda to hers. Tensions that had started at the executive director level soon erupted among the trustees and then among constituents and staff. The two camps became increasingly vocal. Internally, the tension was tremendous, as those loyal to Roger and those to Melinda faced off publicly. When the foundation officer began to hear rumors of problems, he immediately set up a meeting of Roger, Melinda, and the two original board presidents (who were now officers of a single board), and issued a stern warning. If things did not improve, the organization was in danger of losing its funding.

A year later, both Roger and Melinda were gone. The board had failed to resolve the conflict, and with funding in jeopardy, they agreed that they could no longer continue with two directors. Since both Roger and Melinda had lost the confidence of large segments of the board, the only solution was for both to leave. The organization lost a lot of experience, credibility, and good will, and while it retained its main funder, others discontinued their support.

⌄

A shared executive directorship can be successful, although it takes immense effort on the part of the principals and the board to make it work. Frequent and open communication and regular reviews of the directors' performance by the board president or a personnel committee is an absolute must. Especially when only one board is involved, it is easier to establish processes to monitor the relationship and productivity of two individuals carrying out the executive director role. The trustees must be unified in the need to be very much involved in oversight and mindful of the fact that shared executive authority is always potentially problematic.

In the case of an organizational hybrid structure, such as the public library with an affiliated nonprofit that manages its endowment, or the state college with an affiliated nonprofit foundation, the challenge of two executive directors is much more complex, because accountability is bifurcated between two boards. Even if the boards have identical membership (which, on occasion, is the case), there is the problem of two staffs and increased potential for misunderstandings between the two principals (each with authority over a budget and personnel). The need for even more complicated negotiation and communication is paramount.

Lucy was executive director of a city museum. In her previous job, she had run a smaller private museum where she functioned as the sole senior executive responsible for all aspects of the operation including programs, curatorial, administration, fundraising, and other areas. In her new job, the fundraising, function was carried out by an affiliated nonprofit. Lucy understood why this was the case—as a public entity, her museum would not be in a good position to ask for individual donations. While Lucy felt she could easily have run both entities, serving as executive director of both, her supervisor explained that in the past it was decided by the city council that this would not be a sound arrangement.

Lucy's counterpart in the affiliated nonprofit was John. He also carried the title of executive director. He had been around for a long time and was part of what people told Lucy was "the old boys' network." Everyone seemed to like him. But after only two months on the job, Lucy realized he was incompetent.

As she looked at the trends, membership numbers were flagging and had been declining ever since John had taken over as executive director. Record keeping was in a shambles. There was no follow-up when people gave large contributions, so major donors were being lost. Even signature events—long a staple of contributed income—were being mismanaged.

Lucy was confused about how to handle the situation. She and John had to get along; she depended on him for a major part of her budget. Yet, whenever she pointed out there were problems, he always had an excuse. Lucy's offers of help were rebuffed. Confidential complaints to her board were met with comments like, "Sorry, there is nothing we can do. Every time we complain, we are told to mind our business."

In the end, the solution was to bring in a consultant who could evaluate the situation and report on the challenges of the structure, how they could be addressed, and the specific performance of each partner. In the course of the assessment work, the consultant was able to benchmark best-practices in other comparable organizations and come up with what could be considered reasonable if modest expectations in fundraising results. Since John's organization was falling well short of these expectations, his board asked for his resignation, and some problems in organizational structure were addressed once he was gone.

This case shows that it is often impossible for one executive director to point out deficiencies in the other, and outside, objective assistance is often the best solution to an otherwise untenable situation.

Finally, what of the organization that has two staff leaders, one who handles the administrative side of the house, and the other who handles programmatic activities? This situation can be complicated when one of the individuals is considered more important or more prestigious than the other, and this can work against a healthy, balanced relationship.

The example is often given of the symphony orchestra with its music director and executive director. On paper, the executive director carries the title that suggests that he or she is in charge of everything, except the hiring and firing of musicians and the actual events that happen on stage. But in reality, that is often not the case. The music director—often an individual who does not live in the community or travels a great deal—brings star power and charisma. As chief conductor of the orchestra, he (or sometimes she) is the face of the orchestra in the community. Music directors will know other famous musicians and can provide entrée for board members who want to meet them. Keeping this individual happy may trump the good counsel that is provided by the executive director. For example, the music director may have no interest in listening to what a marketing study says about the kind of music that will sell tickets. This individual may convince the board that a tour of Europe would bring prestige to the community, even though the executive director points out that it will dwarf the resources of the orchestra. Who is really in charge when decisions seem to go only one way?

Similar situations can occur in a hospital where ostensibly there is an administrative head called an executive director, but it is the medical director who calls the shots. The board may believe that it is following protocol most of the time when it deals with the executive director on administrative and fundraising issues. On the other hand, the intervention of a medical director can trump all the sound arguments that the executive director makes. It is the doctors, after all, who attract the patients, and the patients (and their insurance companies) who pay the bills, and as the medical director points out, keeping the medical staff happy is crucial to the hospital's quality, research funding, and bottom line.

Thus, there are challenges in divided leadership, even when the portfolios of the leaders are distinct. What can be said is that a board should always assess carefully the arguments made by each party and be sensitive to instances when one individual is poaching on the other's territory. Keeping the balance of power from tilting too much in one direction is a good way to ensure that the overall effectiveness of leadership is protected.

The other requirement, one that has been a consistent theme in virtually every chapter in this book, is clear and thorough communication.

Indeed, good communication was what turned an initially acrimonious relationship between Ingrid and Sam into a positive one, and it was a transformation brokered by a strong and sensitive board president. The two were senior administrators of a major teaching hospital (though neither carried the title executive director, both functioned in an analogous role). Ingrid was the senior medical director. Sam was the chief administrator responsible for finance, marketing, human resources, fundraising, information technology, and related administrative areas. According to the structure, the two positions were co-equal in authority, and both individuals reported directly to the board.

The two clashed in many specific areas, but overshadowing everything was a fundamentally different view of the priorities of the institution. Ingrid felt that Sam just did not understand the educational and service mission of the hospital, and that he and his staff were trying to exert undue influence over decisions about policies that were under her purview. Sam felt that Ingrid lived in a dream world and did not know the realities of what it took to run a hospital in a major city in the twenty-first century.

When the tensions in the relationship started going public, and a newspaper made it the subject of a feature article, the board president took action. He called Ingrid and Sam in separately, explained that the situation was unacceptable, and that while he respected each of them and the work they did, he would not tolerate a situation that damaged the reputation of the institution. He then called them in together and laid out his plan for a solution. He was going to suggest weekly private meetings between the two of them where they could discuss frankly their respective concerns and hash out their differences. Initially, he would join their meeting once a month and would also talk to each separately about how things were going. He also suggested that they look for ways they might occasionally convene senior staff across their respective areas to discuss opportunities and resolve concerns.

The meetings began as proposed and the board president, as promised, met together with Sam and Ingrid and separately on a periodic basis. Pretty soon, these latter meetings with the president became unnecessary, though a semiannual check-in was left on the calendar, and ad hoc meetings were called in special cases where issues needed board input. There were three important outcomes. First, the bickering ended. Second, Ingrid and Sam came to admire one another and became a good working team. Finally, a couple of cross-departmental standing committees of senior staff worked together on issues that could only be resolved through joint effort. By modeling their own cooperative behavior, Sam and Ingrid became an inspiration for their respective staffs.

The lesson from Sam and Ingrid is clear. In cases of divided staff leadership, the goal should always be to harness the combined talents of able individuals who, working together, can increase exponentially the power and effectiveness of an organization.

Questions

1. In cases where the ultimate staff authority is divided, is it clear who is in charge of what? Are job responsibilities clearly stated?

2. If two individuals share a single job, is there a mechanism for board monitoring that ensures the system is working and the individuals are getting along? If they aren't, what is the means for resolving the conflict?

3. In cases where there is a bifurcated organizational structure with separate executive directors, who is in charge of establishing the respective portfolios, responsibilities, and limits of each individual's authority?

4. How can the two sides in a bifurcated structure monitor performance of their own executive director and the other? How can each side have its concerns taken seriously by the other?

5. Does one of the directors command more authority and respect than the other, owing to reputation or area of responsibility? What can be done to fix this problem?

6. Is there a willingness to jointly agree on outside evaluation and monitoring if the system does not seem to be working?

APPENDIX

CREATING THE MAGIC PARTNERSHIP–A CHECKLIST

This concluding appendix offers a diagnostic tool to assess the effectiveness of board–executive director partnerships. It provides material from each of the chapters, including the end-of-chapter questions which, for convenience, are assembled in one place. The material can be used as a self-assessment protocol by individuals within the organization, or it can serve as a guide for use by outside consultants. For more background, the reader should consult the relevant numbered chapter.

Governance, Management, and Leadership in Nonprofit Organizations (Chapter 1)

The roles and responsibilities of trustees are enshrined in both federal and state law, but the law is silent on the topic of executive directors, and their positions can look very different, depending on the organizations for which they work. Good communication about respective tasks and roles is essential in developing a good working relationship.

Questions

1. Do the trustees understand the nature and obligations of trusteeship in nonprofit corporations? Do they understand their accountability to government and the public?

2. How well are the key areas of board responsibility covered among existing trustees?

3. How is the role of executive director defined in the organization? What are the tasks and responsibilities described in the job description?

4. Where are the areas of overlap in the roles of trustees and executive director? Where are the areas of potential conflict?

5. Have communication systems been established that can defuse potential problems?

Whose Organization? (Chapter 2)

The relationship between the executive director and the board is a delicate balance of power in which each can enhance the work of the other in a positive way, or conversely, undermine the other when one side or the other overreaches.

Questions

1. Is there an orientation process for new trustees that introduces them to their role and that of the executive director and staff?

2. Is everyone clear about how legal and fiduciary responsibilities will be properly carried out and what information is needed from the executive director for the board to do its job in this area?

3. Are board members able to convey to the executive director their sense of his or her critically important role in making the organization successful? Do they communicate this in a very public way?

4. Conversely, is the executive director able to acknowledge the important role of the trustees? How often are the words "we" and "our" used instead of "I" and "my" in describing organizational roles and responsibilities?

5. Is the president someone who is sensitive to the issues surrounding interpersonal partnership? Is he or she someone with sufficient respect and authority to take up the issue

with other trustees or the executive director? Are there other trustees who can assist?

6. Are there areas where individual trustees seem to be meddling? How can the executive director be protected in bringing this to the attention of the board and being assured it will be dealt with?

Whose Trustees? (Chapter 3)

While bylaws will stipulate a process for trustee and officer selection that does not involve the executive director, in the real world, executive directors should play at least a behind-the-scenes role in shaping board composition and choosing officers.

Questions

1. What are the official processes for identifying, nominating, and electing new trustees in the organization? What do the bylaws specify in terms of who is involved in the process?

2. If the appointments to the organization's board are made by another entity or individual, are there ways that existing board members and the executive director can influence those decisions?

3. In the case of self-perpetuating boards, are there formal and open ways that the executive director can be invited to participate in the process of making suggestions and vetting candidates, even if some of the discussions need to be restricted to trustees only?

4. Are there more private ways the executive director can get his or her views taken into account? Is there anyone on the nominating committee who can quietly solicit the executive director's views, with or without attribution?

5. How comfortable are the president and executive director in having frank, private conversations about the performance of current trustees and officers? Can both secure reliable assurances that neither will be quoted without permission?

6. What are the processes by which officers are selected? How active can the executive director be in this process?

But I Have Always Done That Job (Chapter 4)

As organizations grow and become more professionalized, it can be tricky to manage the adjustment for trustees who have been active as working volunteers. Trustees who may have assisted with management functions when an organization is young and small must evolve into board members concerned primarily with policy, planning, and fundraising. The bumpy road can and should be greatly eased by an effective and sensitive executive director.

Questions

1. Is the organization too small for an executive director at this time? What key indicators would signal that one is needed?
2. What steps must take place for a first-time executive director to be successful? How can an existing volunteer leader be helpful without being intrusive, while ultimately stepping aside?
3. What support will the board provide to help an executive director professionalize the staff of a growing organization, replacing volunteers with paid staff?
4. How fully cognizant are the trustees of their governance responsibilities? Has organizational growth shifted their roles? Who is primarily responsible for reeducating them about what will be required of them in the future?
5. Is there a glide path for volunteers (including board members) who are not comfortable with change, helping them transition to new roles?
6. What are the main talking points as trustees and the executive director talk to board prospects about governance responsibilities in the organization?

So You Want My Advice . . . (Chapter 5)

While trustees are often recruited for knowledge and expertise, a board must have balance with an emphasis on financial skills, giving and getting abilities, and other legal aspects of trusteeship. Those only with expertise may meddle in areas that are best left to staff. Soliciting advice but not being beholden to "experts" often requires coordinated efforts by both executive directors and boards.

Questions

1. How well are the four "w's " (wealth, workers, worriers, and wisdom) represented on the board? Where are the gaps?
2. Have the president and the executive director had an opportunity to speak frankly about getting more balance on the board, and is there a mechanism for doing so?
3. Are board members who are knowledgeable about programs and activities too involved in day-to-day decisions? Is there a mechanism by which the executive director can safely and privately raise concerns about the problem?
4. Is there an experienced and skilled president (or other trustee) who can help remind those who are acting as shadow staff that this is not an appropriate trustee role?
5. Is there a committee structure that allows trustees who have in-depth knowledge and interest about an area to have an opportunity to express their views and make suggestions? If so, is it made clear to them that their role is advisory only?
6. Are there ways that important decisions can be vetted early, prior to the time they are voted on by the full board, to ensure that they will not be held up?

Picking a Winner (with a Little Help) (Chapter 6)

It is not easy to identify and recruit an ideal candidate as executive director who will inspire, lead, and work well with trustees, the staff, and the community. It requires a good process and focus by the trustees. Sometimes, an outgoing executive director, if respected and respectful, can assist.

Questions

1. How well-equipped is the board to identify and recruit a new executive director? Is there a succession plan in place?

2. Are there any staff members who could conceivably be future executive directors in the organization? Are there any processes in place to nurture them for possible future leadership?

3. Has the outgoing executive director provided a reasonable amount of notice? If not, can anything be done to encourage more time before his or her departure?

4. Has a proper interim administrative structure been set up to ensure appropriate leadership during a possible transitional period between an outgoing and incoming executive director?

5. Is it appropriate to ask the outgoing executive director for assistance in the search for his or her successor? Is the relationship such that the board feels comfortable making the request?

6. If yes, in what ways can the outgoing executive director assist in the identification of a successor? Providing a vision of the future? Identifying desired qualities needed in a successor? Providing a list of actual candidates? Vetting candidates? Speaking confidentially and honestly to candidates about the position?

Turning on the Spigot (Chapter 7)

An effective (and somewhat invisible) partnership between an executive director and board member can entice some trustees to give money ... and others to give more generously. Though technically it is the board's job to police and incentivize its own fundraising habits, there are many ways the executive director can help behind the scenes.

Questions

1. Is the board fulfilling its giving requirements? Is there 100 percent participation? Is the giving level high enough?

2. Are there members of the board who, for one reason or another, are not required to give? Do the reasons for this nonparticipation appear to be valid ones, or should the policy be changed?

3. Are there explicit policies in place about giving? What are they? How and where are they expressed? How are they shared with existing and prospective board members?

4. Is there a minimum giving requirement? Is there a goal for the board as a whole? How do these change (and presumably rise) over time?

5. Are there board members who are willing to take on the problem of inadequate trustee giving? Are there ways the executive director can be helpful in the process, without jeopardizing important board relationships?

6. What more convincing arguments can be made to get board members to give? What incentives can be created to ensure that they give at the level at which they are capable?

Cracking the Whip: Getting Trustees to Fundraise (Chapter 8)

In many organizations, the challenge is not in getting trustees to give money. It is getting them to fulfill their responsibility as fundraisers. There are many incentivizing roles the executive director can play in building partnerships with the board leadership to solve the problem.

Questions

1. Is there a general policy that trustees in the organization should be involved in fundraising? How is the requirement stated? If a policy does not exist, is the topic regularly discussed? Should an explicit written policy be developed?

2. If and when trustees refuse to get involved in fundraising, what reasons do they give? What are some strategies to address their concerns and fears?

3. Are fundraising assignments documented, scheduled, and put into a master calendar? Is there a system of monitoring, reminding, and addressing situations where work is not getting completed? Does the executive director get assistance from trustees in helping to deal with problem situations?

4. How are board members oriented to the comprehensive nature of fundraising and the many opportunities to do different tasks associated with it? Are there special orientation sessions for new trustees? Are there ways that individuals can opt for those areas where they will be most comfortable and successful?

5. Are there training opportunities for those who are willing to be solicitors? Are these sessions set up to address their anxieties? Are there experienced trustees or staff willing to accompany inexperienced solicitors on calls, at least initially, until they have had some success?

6. Is the executive director sufficiently experienced and confident to carry out the functions involved in getting board members to become involved in fundraising? If not, are there ways that he or she can get more help?

Understanding and Overseeing the Finances (Chapter 9)

The board treasurer, the executive director, the finance director, the finance committee of the board, the investment committee, and the executive committee all have to be on top of the finances. At certain points, all the trustees have to be well-informed. As part of an effective partnership, everyone's role has to be well-understood.

Questions

1. How well-informed are the trustees about finances in the organization? Do they have sufficient information to make

good decisions and carry out their fiduciary responsibilities? If not, what improvements can be made?

2. Is the board satisfied with the financial reports they receive? Do these reports include both sufficient detail and appropriate summary information that everyone can understand?

3. How active is the treasurer and the finance committee? Are they able to digest detailed information and make informed recommendations? Is there appropriate information sharing with the executive committee, such that its members can decide what needs to be forwarded to the full board for review and votes?

4. How well do the treasurer, the board chair, the finance director (if there is one), and the executive director work together? In what areas can the relationships be improved?

5. Does the executive director have a proper understanding of the finances and the financial management activities of the staff? Does he or she serve as a proper conduit between the financial activities of the staff and board?

6. If the executive director's financial responsibilities are delegated to another staff person, is there sufficient communication, so that the staff leader is well-informed and able to respond to questions and concerns of the board?

Planning for the Future (Chapter 10)

A planning process is an opportunity to get everyone involved in thinking about the future. A challenge is to come up with a workable plan when there are many divergent views. It will take coordination between the executive director, who generally has the most detailed information, and the trustees, who hold the power to approve or disapprove the plan, to agree on a process to build organizational consensus.

Questions

1. How inclusive should a planning process be for the organization? Besides trustees and staff, are there others whose

opinions matter—funders, volunteers, constituents, community and field leaders? How will they be involved?

2. How involved will the board be in the process? What role will the board president play? Is there a planning committee that will solicit and represent the views of the trustees?

3. How will the staff be involved? How can the executive director ensure that the detailed knowledge and experience of the staff enriches and informs the process?

4. Will a consultant be used? If so, how can this individual help bring about consensus and move the process along on schedule?

5. What is the timeline for final approval? What steps will lead to a final vote? Will it be necessary or desirable to utilize a consent calendar approach?

No Surprises, Please (Chapter 11)

Effective communication is essential between an executive director and the board. This means passing on critical information and providing feedback. It also means that the executive director will seek authorization for major new initiatives or important decisions, while the board will not delay in providing answers. Feedback on each other's performance—both formally and informally—is also critical.

Questions

1. Does the executive director routinely pass on important information to the board? Does he or she seek permission for pursuing new areas of activity that are part of the board's purview?

2. What are the mechanisms for communicating with the board to ensure that information will be assessed and passed on to the trustees as necessary? Aside from the board president, are there others with whom the executive director should communicate in specific situations?

3. Has the board done everything possible to respond quickly to executive director requests when important opportunities or concerns have to be addressed?

4. How can the annual performance review be used as a way to ensure that there is good communication between the executive director and the board?

5. What are the topics and situations in which boards need to preserve confidentiality of communication? Are there ways that they can diffuse anxiety on the part of the executive director by being open about these areas?

6. When personnel issues are being discussed, is the board open about how the process will work and how and when the executive director will be informed of the results?

Coming and Going (Chapter 12)

The better the executive director, the more likely some other organizations will try to entice him or her away. But there are many incentives and actions that can keep an executive director loyal, and the board can play a critical role in making the individual feel that staying is the best course of action.

Questions

1. How valuable is the executive director to the organization? How high a price in time, money, prestige, or community opinion would be paid if the executive director left?

2. Has any effort been made to determine what comparable positions pay both locally and nationally? If the current salary and benefits are well below par, has anything been done to start rectifying the problem? Has any thought been given to a deferred benefits package?

3. Has the board considered offering release time, either for national meetings or a sabbatical, to the executive director?

4. Does the executive director have proper help in the office? Does he or she spend too much time on mundane matters because of inadequate support?
5. If the executive director has had a long tenure or was promoted from within, is there a procedure for regularly assessing whether he or she is being treated fairly?
6. What other perks that do not cost money have been considered to reward the executive director? Are there ways that appreciation can be made obvious and made public?

Not Soon Enough (Chapter 13)

Firing an incompetent executive director is hard enough. But much more challenging is encouraging a long-time, successful executive director that it is time to move on without the public acrimony accompanying a firing. There are proven techniques for doing both.

Questions

1. Is the executive director's job description up-to-date? Does it spell out job responsibilities and expectations?
2. What is the process by which the executive director is reviewed by the board? Does it occur at least annually? Are job expectations set out for the coming year?
3. Is there a personnel manual that spells out the procedures for dismissal? If not, is there some other official document where this process is spelled out?
4. In addition to illegal activity, are there documented areas and policies that spell out activities that are grounds for dismissal?
5. Is the board prepared to have a conversation about when it may be time for a long-time executive director to move on?
6. What incentives can the board offer an executive director for a quiet, orderly resignation, and what will it expect in return?

Getting Help (Chapter 14)

Sometimes, even an effective board and a good executive director end up at an impasse and are stymied. At other times, otherwise effective executive directors have gaps in abilities or knowledge that need to be addressed. Help can often come from the outside, leading to a much more harmonious working relationship.

Questions

1. Is there a regular system in place for identifying problems in the relationship between the board and the executive director? If not, how can the problem be addressed?

2. Can this system also pick out shortcomings in the relationship between the executive director and the staff? If not, how can that challenge be addressed?

3. What diagnostic tools are available for pinpointing problems in the performance of the executive director? Are there triggers that lead to the scheduling of special sessions if they cannot wait for regularly scheduled performance evaluations?

4. What various actions are possible when problems are identified with the executive director's performance? Who is responsible for working out the steps with the executive director that can lead to improved performance?

5. What kinds of outside assistance might be appropriate to help an executive director improve performance? Is the board prepared to pay to secure this kind of help?

6. How might the board or the staff or both be productively drawn into the executive director counseling process?

Bad News . . . and Good (Chapter 15)

It is important to have an official spokesperson within the organization when important information has to be conveyed to the community and to the media. Especially in a time of crisis, messages have to be carefully crafted and there needs to be internal discipline regarding rules and protocols to be worked out ahead of time so things go smoothly when the pressure is on. Good news, too, offers special communication opportunities.

Questions

1. Does the organization have a formal communications plan, including a plan for crisis communications as well as good news, that is shared with the board?

2. Are there guidelines about who is the official spokesperson for the organization? Are there situations where it could be more than one person?

3. What constitutes information that should only go through official channels in order to be properly communicated to the community? On other matters, if the board or staff is called for comment, what is the policy with regard to their permission to provide information?

4. Is there a crisis protocol that ensures a message will be crafted quickly, the board and staff notified, and a single individual ready to step forward as the message point person?

5. Are people sufficiently aware of the possibility of deferring awkward decisions by invoking the need to consult with the board? What is the follow-through and board-notification process when this occurs?

6. Has sufficient thought been given to how good news is delivered to the community? Are board members selected for this task? Are there public speaking opportunities where board members can be given a chance to shine?

Oh No, Not Another Meeting (Chapter 16)

The secret of planning and executing great board meetings is an aspect of the effective partnership of the board leadership and the executive director. Creating the agenda, limiting the time of the business meeting and sticking to a timetable, preventing surprises and unbridled controversy, and giving people an incentive to attend (including fun and interesting topics) are all part of a good design.

Questions

1. Are board meetings carefully planned with meaningful and important agenda items that can be decided without undue controversy?
2. Is there a committee system that allows detailed and controversial information to be discussed and vetted in advance by selected trustees and staff so they are able to come before the full board with committee endorsement?
3. Is material sent out in advance so that routine or detailed information does not have to take up valuable board-meeting time?
4. How well do the executive director and the executive committee work together to ensure that board meetings focus on the important issues?
5. Is there a mechanism to determine how votes will go before meetings take place? Is the president prepared to turn an action item into a discussion item if decisions cannot be reached in the allotted time?
6. How often does the board convene to discuss longer-range and controversial issues? Is the executive director properly utilized in planning these meetings? Are outside resource people used? Are these sessions clearly differentiated from business meetings?

How Many Boards Do We Have? (Chapter 17)

Hybrid entities (public-private partnerships) that have both a public sector board and a private nonprofit board create special governance and management challenges. While an executive director generally only works for one of these entities, he or she may bear some accountability to each board. Negotiating complex relationships both legally and interpersonally takes great skill.

Questions

1. Is the organization a public or private sector entity? Is it part of a divisional structure with multiple boards? Does it have an independently linked, private nonprofit support organization with its own board?

2. Is the executive director a public or private employee, and to whom does he or she report? If there are multiple reports, is it clear who has ultimate authority over the executive director's continued tenure in the position?

3. Who evaluates the executive director? If there are multiple processes, are they coordinated?

4. If there are multiple boards, is there cross membership such that public members serve on the private board, and vice versa? What other strategies are there for regular communication?

5. What is the budget process? Who is ultimately responsible for approving the budget? Are there ways that all parties can have input into the process?

6. How strong is communication between all parties? Is the private board in regular communication with public board members and the executive director? Are private board members party to important decisions outside of fundraising, even if they do not have voting privileges on such matters?

How Many Directors Do We Have? (Chapter 18)

Some organizations have more than one executive director, either because two people share the job, or because in a bifurcated structure, each unit has an executive director. In other situations, two directors may have different titles and areas of responsibility, but each is directly accountable to the board and neither has authority over the other. The board or boards play a major role in ensuring that these relationships can work effectively.

Questions

1. In cases where the ultimate staff authority is divided, is it clear who is in charge of what? Are job responsibilities clearly stated?

2. If two individuals share a single job, is there a mechanism for board monitoring that ensures the system is working and the individuals are getting along? If they aren't, what is the means for resolving the conflict?

3. In cases where there is a bifurcated organizational structure with separate executive directors, who is in charge of establishing the respective portfolios, responsibilities, and limits of each individual's authority?

4. How can the two sides in a bifurcated structure monitor performance of their own executive director and the other? How can each side have its concerns taken seriously by the other?

5. Does one of the directors command more authority and respect than the other, owing to reputation or area of responsibility? What can be done to fix this problem?

6. Is there a willingness to jointly agree on outside evaluation and monitoring if the system does not seem to be working?

INDEX

ABOUT THE AUTHOR

Dr. Thomas Wolf has spent over four decades working in the nonprofit world, serving as both executive director and a trustee for several organizations. An internationally recognized consultant, he founded the Cambridge office of WolfBrown in 1983 and prior to that served as the founding director of the New England Foundation for the Arts for seven years. Wolf holds a doctorate from Harvard and he has taught at both Harvard and Boston University. He is the author of a popular textbook, *Managing a Nonprofit Organization* (now in a fourth, updated 21st century edition) and has also written *How to Connect with Donors and Double the Money You Raise*, among many other books. He lives in Cambridge, Massachusetts.

Books from Allworth Press

Allworth Press is an imprint of Skyhorse Publishing, Inc. Selected titles are listed below.

Branding for Nonprofits
By DK Holland (6 x 9, 208 pages, paperback, $19.95)

Brand Thinking and Other Noble Pursuits
By Debbie Millman (6 x 9, 336 pages, paperback, $19.95)

Guide to Getting Arts Grants
By Ellen Liberatori (6 x 9, 272 pages, paperback, $19.95)

How to Win Grants: 101 Winning Strategies
By Alan Silver (5 ½ x 8 ¼, 168 pages, paperback, $12.95)

Infectious: How to Connect Deeply and Unleash the Energetic Leader Within
By Achim Nowak (5 ½ x 8 ¼, 224 pages, paperback, $19.95)

Legal Guide to Social Media: Rights and Risks for Businesses and Entrepreneurs
By Kimberly A. Houser (6 x 9, 208 pages, paperback, $19.95)

The Pocket Small Business Owner's Guide to Business Plans
By Brian Hill and Dee Power (5 ¼ x 8 ¼, 224 pages, paperback, $14.95)

The Pocket Legal Companion to Copyright
By Lee Wilson (5 x 7 ½, 336 pages, paperback, $16.95)

The Pocket Legal Companion to Patents
By Carl Battle (5 x 7 ½, 384 pages, paperback, $16.95)

The Pocket Legal Companion to Trademark
By Lee Wilson (5 x 7 ½, 320 pages, paperback, $16.95)

The Pocket Small Business Owner's Guide to Negotiating
By Richard Weisgrau (5 ¼ x 8 ¼, 224 pages, paperback, $14.95)

Your Living Trust and Estate Plan, Fifth Edition
By Harvey J. Platt (6 x 9, 368 pages, paperback, $16.95)

To see our complete catalog or to order online, please visit *www.allworth.com*.